"The message comes through loud-and-clear! A superb job!"
>Bill Scott, Rocky Mountain Bureau Chief, Aviation-Week

"Great job! I'm amazed! *The System* is helping me articulate some things I have believed and experienced but have not consciously thought about."
>Dr. John Bransford, Professor of Education, College of Education, University of Washington

"Really Great Book!!!"
>David Shaw, Sr. Managing Dir/CEO, Global Business Analysis

"Knocks 'The Goal' off the field!"
>Ian Wigston, Thoughtforge, London England

"Brings the problems down to where the rubber meets the road!"
>M.B. Lockhart

"A fresh and personal approach to business, commerce, and the human experience!"
>Michael C. Richey

"It is a pleasure to read a novel that so succinctly lays out the most important ingredients for problem solving in modern times. *The System* is certain to be a powerful tool in helping others effect change."
>Cinda Russell-Reese, Ed.D., Chief Education Officer, Russell Certified Learning

"Amazingly brilliant, provides strategically practical global leadership in intergenerational, intercultural workforce development for economic and community stakeholders. Can hardly put it down!"

Sandra Greenough, CHRP, Life, Career & Leadership Passion Coach, President, Greenough & Associates Inc.

"Thought provoking and inspiring. Elegantly helps the reader see the system by pointing to the connections right in front of us."

Robert Rasmussen, Partner, LEGO SERIOUS PLAY in Americas

"A wonderful blueprint for connecting educators, business and community leaders, with their community."

Mike O'Connor, MA. Educ., AVID Co-Ordinator

The System

Volume I

Seeking the Soul of Commerce

By

Rick Stephens, and
Elane V. Scott

With

Glen Knape, and
Robert A. Davis

Preparation Press
Whittier, CA

The System

Volume I

Seeking the Soul of Commerce

By Rick Stephens, and Elane V. Scott,
With Glen Knape, and Robert A. Davis

Prepublication Review edition, 2006

Preparing the way

Preparation Press
Whittier, CA, USA
www.preparationpress.com

Cover Art by Georgia Lambert

ISBN 0-9760084-3-2

Dedicated to the Memory of

Dr. Stephen Glenn

Acknowledgement

The authors gratefully acknowledge the contributions of the groups and individuals whose efforts made this work possible.

Disclaimer

While this is a work of fiction, it is based on real work being done by real people.

T*he ideas, experiences, and data at the heart of the text*, around which the characters and their adventures revolve, *are entirely real.*

The characters included herein are fictional, and any resemblance between them and real persons, living or deceased, is purely coincidental. The opinions expressed herein do not necessarily represent those of the authors, the publisher, or anyone else.

Table of Contents

Dramatis Personae

Alice Allegren: Wife of Leonard, mother of Bruce.
Amanda Caldwell: Director of the Terra H.R. team.
Anna Somers: Editor of the Chantilly Chronicle.
Barbara Ellis: Assistant H.R. Manager at Terra.
Bill Alperton: A tech guy at Terra.
Bill Rutherford: Engineering Manager a Terra.
Bruce Aguilera: Leonard's son, a high school student with ADD.
Bhupath (Bud) Vatave, Dr., City Councilman
Chantilly College: Local two-year college.
Chantilly Stars: Chantilly College basketball team
Chelsea University: Local four-year private University.
Clint Samuels: Terra's Waste Water Treatment Mgr.
Cunningham, Mrs.: Principal of Madison Elementary.
Dan Blank: Previous CEO of Terra Waste Management
Dennis Aiken: Terra's Communications Director
Donna Aguilera: Wife of George, mother of Elizabeth, grandmother of Dusty.
E.T. Stroud: A local business leader.
Dusty: Grandson of George and Donna, son of Elizabeth.
Elizabeth (Lizabeth): Daughter of George and Donna, of Dusty.
Edra Brode, Dr.: School Superintendent
Gedisman, Dr.: Physician in charge of Bruce's treatment.
George Aguilera: Director of R&D at Terra Waste Management, husband of Donna, father of Elizabeth, grandfather of Dusty.
Gill Chandler: Reporter, National Waste Mgmnt Journal
Houston Campbell: Local hi-tech cattle rancher.
Isabel: Central American girl sponsored by McKenzie.
Jane Dawson: Leonard's secretary/office assistant
Janet Reams: Curriculum Director for Chantilly Unified
Jason: Head of Advertising Sales at the Chronicle

Jennifer (Jenny) Henson: Student at Madison Elementary, later an employee at Terra.

Joe Delaney: U.S. Congressman from Utah.

KBCT: Local T.V. station.

Larry Spandle: Director, Academy of Engineering

Leonard Allegren: CEO of Terra, Husband of Alice, father of Bruce.

Lyceum Foundation: An organization of stakeholders in the local community.

Marci Baker: Director Community Relations (C.R.) at Terra.

Marcus: Student at Madison Elementary School.

Marsha Stone: Student at Madison Elementary School.

Martha Flemming: Lyceum member, parent of the current Chantilly High valedictorian.

Maureen McMahon, Dr.: President of Chelsea University

McKenzie Jordan: Reporter for the Chantilly Chronicle, community commentator at KCCT, and former teacher.

Michael Hernandez, Dr.: President of the American Science Teacher's Association.

Ricardo Valentino, Dr.: Local pediatrician.

Ron (Ronnie): Student at Madison Elementary School.

Rose McPherson, Dr.: President of Chantilly College

Rusty Hawkins: Director of Waste Management Engineering at Terra.

SJ Dakota: Conservative Republican Lyceum member.

Dr. Stephen Glenn: Retired research psychologist.

Ted Bruer: President, Chantilly Chamber of Commerce.

Terra Waste Management (Terra): A $3 Billion company.

Tom: Controller, Terra Waste Management.

Trevor: Mayor of Chantilly, Immediate Past Chair of the Lyceum, and Past President of Chantilly Capital.

Wheaton High: Local high school where McKenzie was the journalism teacher.

Winston-Kellogg: Giant media conglomerate that purchases KBCT

Introduction

Seeking the Soul of Commerce

Introduction

Americans have always been recognized for their ingenuity and ability to do business anywhere in the world. One
of their major strengths has been a willingness to respond
to change quickly, with a wealth of creativity and drive to
adapt to that change. This is the basis for success in a free
market economy.

Though not always comfortable, the speed with which
those changes have been adopted by the mass populace has
allowed America to hold a global leadership position for
some time. That position is now at risk. The foundation for
adaptability has been America's education system. *For purposes of this book, that education system encompasses both
the formal classroom and the life of the individual outside
that classroom.* That foundation is now at risk.

Today, America has top-notch leaders working and
leading in every sector of its economy. But not until very
recently has the pipeline that feeds that talent become
of serious concern to those who rely on it to plan for the
future. There have been signs for some time that the
education system, the core of building good, strong leaders and skilled members for the future workforce, has
been skidding. While more and more evidence has become visible recently, the first empirical signs appeared
in 1963. Billions of dollars have been spent trying to stop
the decline, but the tide has not yet changed. Why not?

There are many reasons why today's students step
into the world of work unprepared. But to see the real
reasons for such dramatic change we must look further
than what happens in our classrooms. We must begin to
be more inclusive and focus on what happens throughout
an individual's life. Preparing for the future world of work
is not about gathering, assimilating, and regurgitating

information in a closed environment. It is about the development of the body, the mind, and the soul, and about strategically integrating information from each for survival and growth, and for adding value in the global marketplace. When the majority lived on farms, youngsters used to hone their thinking skills with hands-on jobs that demanded their attention. They bailed hay, took care of animals, and played a key role in growing and harvesting food in harmony with the seasons. On a daily basis they routinely made critical decisions that impacted their own individual life and the lives of those around them. In some cases there were immediate, life-threatening consequences for failure to carry their share of the workload. Typically, knowledge was learned and put to immediate use in personal ways and for the benefit of those who lived together.

Today, failure to perform is seldom met with life-threatening consequences, and thus, for most, life is different. Technology, innovation, creativity and determination of the current workforce have created a safer and much "easier" society, along with a different world of challenges.

The rate of knowledge creation has increased exponentially, and with it technology has provided accessibility and acquisition to that knowledge beyond life-sustaining actions. In addition, knowledge or information is no longer limited to a few. It is available to the many. Years ago information *was* power, but today, information is just that, information.

The rate of knowledge creation and information exchange has had dramatic implications for existing educational processes. It's nearly impossible for the educational "system" (as it is commonly called) to keep pace. That said, education is not failing society, society is failing the education process, because education that matters does not happen just in the classroom.

Introduction

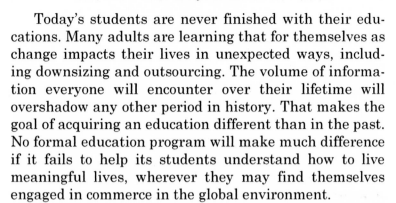

Today's students are never finished with their educations. Many adults are learning that for themselves as change impacts their lives in unexpected ways, including downsizing and outsourcing. The volume of information everyone will encounter over their lifetime will overshadow any other period in history. That makes the goal of acquiring an education different than in the past. No formal education program will make much difference if it fails to help its students understand how to live meaningful lives, wherever they may find themselves engaged in commerce in the global environment.

There is no doubt that some types of information provide a competitive advantage. But those who will regularly achieve success, and maintain it, are those who are able to use their critical, creative thinking skills to quickly and continuously integrate information. They can move efficiently to meet market demands for products and services as well as serve the human thirst for excellence in development at all levels.

Thus, knowledge alone is not power. Thinking skills that create value are what *become* power. Those skills cannot be memorized. They are developed from life experience, without which, they cannot be applied. Those who gain knowledge and achieve understanding through their living experiences, along with profound knowledge, will be the ones to move us forward from the "*Information Age*" to the "*Age of Critical Creative Thinking*."

This book is about a journey. Two people shared a background of knowledge and experience acquired over more than 70 years. Their insights and ideas have been drawn from every major economic sector, to create the story of this journey, the journey we must all take if we are to create communities, nations, and societies that will be successful in the Age of Critical Creative Thinking. It is the journey of discovery, about how people develop, learn, get educated in the new economic environment, and apply what they have learned for those who follow. It is a journey about communication, collaboration, and integration of knowledge, thoughts, values, wisdom and vision. And it is a journey that requires us to recognize that the future ain't what it used to be.

In the late 50s the best advice a stock broker could give to his client was to "buy and hold." Today, in a changing world, that advice would be about recognizing and managing change as quickly and deftly as economic structures change. Changing the way in which investment advice is given is not the problem. Changing the way investors are in the habit of investing is. The implications for education are the same.

Look at the new economic structures all around and ask if what students need to know to live and thrive in them could possibly be taught in a system that has changed little in 50 years? Everyone who has a stake in the lives of tomorrow's youth must talk together as never before. It is time for a whole new understanding of what the demands will be on tomorrow's citizens and what needs to be done now to prepare the way.

Continuous tweaking of classroom curriculum or the way teachers deliver information has not yielded significant enough change for students in 40 years. How can continuous testing of the results of that information delivery system alone tell us what their potential for success will be in the future?

In *The System*, readers encounter the foundational knowledge that shaped our nation's thoughts and ideas before World War II, and discover the tools for their own journey—the journey to understand the broader relationships between and responsibilities of business, government, education, media, community, and health organizations in developing capable people for the future who are:

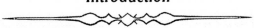
- Economically self sufficient
- Active participants in the process of governance
- Able to effectively communicate and interact with others
- Passionate about learning, unlearning and re-learning
- Focused on the future

For us, the journey started several years ago, after listening to a remarkable presentation where the speaker discussed a set of critical business issues—mostly customer / supplier relationships. The speaker also talked about one issue dealing with people, expressing concern about whether or not there would be enough of them in the future with the right skills to meet the needs of the industry folks he was addressing.

It was clear at that time that the customer/supplier issues would be solved. After all, short-term business success was at stake. But when it came to the issue about people, business could be called upon to describe its people issue in terms of needs, but "educators" would be asked to solve the problem of how to get them there. It was at that point that the alarm was sounded and the journey began.

A partnership was formed between two people with a common passion for creating successful people for the future, but who had very dissimilar backgrounds. One was a business and industry outsider who understood communications and the world of media, the education system, community organizations and human development. The other was a business leader with many years of experience leading national and international businesses of all sizes, working with government contracts, and health service organizations. Although the story line is fictitious, the characters throughout are based on the lives of real people.

This is the beginning of the story and a journey in

search of the place in life's economic marketplace where all human activity has value, where we can find and reveal the true meaning of commerce—about the relationships, about exchange, and about the role commerce plays in keeping a society moving forward.

For the authors, commerce is more than business transactions for goods and services. Engaging in commerce is the way in which we as individuals, communities, and nations engage in society on a daily basis. What we choose to do with the resources we have reveals who we are from the inside out. What we value is expressed by what we are willing to exchange for what we want and need. In that moment when we finalize the terms of each exchange, we further refine the culture of commerce. Together we can innovate and create an environment and educational "system" that will develop our citizens for a future that is ever changing, increasingly complex, and more competitive than ever before. In doing so we begin a journey that transforms the *soul of commerce.*

Many might expect this to be a non-fiction book, but it is in fact a fictional story based on real work being done by real people. Thus the *ideas, experiences, and data at the heart of the text,* around which the characters and their adventures revolve, *are entirely real.* We hope you will recognize yourself on this journey, because more than likely you and/or members of your community are facing the same issues, the same challenges and the same concerns as those who live in the fictional community of Chantilly. We hope this book helps provide a perspective and sense of possibilities that will help all of us develop citizens who have the capacity and capability to innovate and thrive in our future world.

Rick Stephens and Elane V. Scott

Prologue

"It is the little creature that is the bearer of the divine miracle, for this little creature is nothing less than the creative individual, and it is under his guidance that the human race makes progress on its journey through history."
Erich Neumann

Seeking the Soul of Commerce

Prologue

Leonard strode from his office toward the nearest exit, already visualizing the upcoming session with his wife and their son's school counselor. Among many other problems, their son Bruce was still 'forgetting' to hand in his homework and his school was running out of patience. Leonard was so preoccupied with parental self-doubt, and worries for his son, that when a familiar voice called, "Mr. Allegren!" he walked past several doors before stopping.

Leonard sighed, retraced his steps, put on his business face, and walked into the "Community & Educational Resources" office. The small room was crowded with members of his "crisis team." Behind her desk, her forehead creased in disapproval, the usually perky Barbara Ellis was scanning the Chantilly Chronicle.

Dennis Aiken, from H.R., was slouched in the visitor's chair to Leonard's left. Dennis caught Leonard's eye, nodded toward Barbara and said, "Have you seen this? It's today's."

Bill Rutherford from R&D, and Clint Samuels, the Waste Water Treatment Manager, were seated to Leonard's right. Bill recrossed his legs and nodded, while Clint remained bent over—wiping yellowish-gray ooze from the side of his boot. Bill said, "It's that Jordan woman again, Clint brought it in."

Clint straightened, slid the stained cloth into a plastic bag, tucked the bag into his overalls and said, "My wife pointed it out this morning, but I didn't have a chance to give it to Dennis until after lunch."

Leonard glanced up at the ceiling, exhaled and asked, "What does she say this time?"

Barbara snorted, looked up, held out the folded paper and said, "It says every business in Chantilly shares the same workforce problem but *we* get the headline. Why would she do that? Here."

Leonard Allegren, CEO of Terra Waste Management, took the paper, turned it right side up and read,

Terra Wasting Away

Chantilly—Local economy threatened by shortage of skilled workers!

Local officials and businessmen voiced heightened concern for their ability to meet their own workforce needs, following Friday's announcement by Bon Vitale, the French pharmaceutical company, that Chantilly is the first choice for the location of a new plant.

Ted Bruer, President of the Chantilly Chamber of Commerce, told the Chronicle that, "No business leader in this tri-state area would deny the economic value of a new company in our area, but far too many of us are already having problems meeting our needs for a quality, skilled workforce. Hundreds of skilled, well-paying jobs are already going begging in the tri-county region.

"State political and business leaders preach the economic need for more, well-paying jobs, but jobs alone are not the problem for us at the local level. There are plenty of good jobs now, and more coming, but we can't fill them because the available workers don't have the needed skills."

According to Patricia Sullivan, of the Bruer County office of the E.D.D., "The real problem is that we can't replace the retiring Boomers. Our population isn't growing, it's aging—the average employee is 48—and it's becoming increasingly difficult for our employers to replace high skilled retiring workers."

Barbara Ellis, H.R. Manager for Terra Waste Management, said, "The real problem for us is the quality of the applicants. Four out of five don't have the skill sets we need. Even basic math, reading, and communication skills are missing for many applicants."

Prologue

An international leader in municipal, industrial, and agricultural waste management, Terra is by far the largest employer in the County, and is a cornerstone of the local economy. Twelve of their key employees have retired in the last year, and thus far they have been able to replace only two of them. In the past year, fully one third of the available, highly skilled, technical positions have remained open for five months or longer, and the hiring delay is growing. Terra's crisis in filling new hourly positions is shared by our smaller companies.

A recent study conducted by Chelsea University, and financed by the Lyceum Foundation, further illustrates the problem.

The study surveyed employers in Bruer, Alpine, Sul, and Kokemot Counties. Sixty-three percent of respondents agreed that there was a growing skills deficit, and 53 percent said it was having a serious effect on their business.

"Compounding the declining basic skill levels is the increasing complexity of new jobs, creating a widening skills deficit. This skills deficit is already impacting local business and industry and impeding their ability to focus on growth. When local companies can't find what they need in their communities, they are forced to relocate to wherever they can find employees with the necessary skills, at the right price. The alternative is to raise salaries to attract those with the right skills set, but that makes a company non-competitive." said Professor Andrew Barnhoffer, who supervised the survey.

Professor Barnhoffer indicated that the problem appears to be pervasive, with all regions of the country experiencing the same types of workforce problems, with no simple, identifiable cause or silver bullet answers.

Contributors: Staff Writer McKenzie Jordan

Hours later, Leonard slumped into the bucket seat of his Jag, beside Alice, and sat staring at the thick packet, "Recommendations for the A.D.D. Child," that the school's representatives had just spent two hours reviewing with them. Alice's eyes brimmed with the unshed tears of conflicting emotions. After nearly a minute of silence, Alice asked, "Did we do something wrong?"

Leonard reached past the polished oak shift knob, gently placed his hand on hers and said, "No one could have been a better mother."

Welcoming his firm hand, Alice raised her head and demanded, "What do we do now?

After a few more moments of shared silence, Alice said, "I won't give our son drugs."

Leonard replied, "I know. It can't be the only option; I'll call Dr. Gedissman first thing tomorrow."

Alice asked, "What do we tell Bruce?"

Leonard replied, "That we've had a meeting and we're trying to figure out what's going on. We don't know what it means yet."

Leonard pressed the start button. The engine purred to life, and he drove them home, immersed in worry and doubt.

It just didn't make any sense. Sure, there was a medical reason behind A.D.D., a scientific explanation. But what confounded him, what insulted his sense of order, was that this happened in his world. He'd always been so careful, so disciplined, as a father and husband. He'd been so diligent about his family's welfare, provided every advantage for Bruce. It just defied logic that his son was faltering, on the brink of failure.

At that moment, the science and medicine didn't matter to him. What worried him was how the whole, blasted thing had so unexpectedly and ruthlessly ambushed him and his family.

Chapter 1

Focus on the Future

What You Learn First Stays With You the Longest

"The tower-building termites of Africa and Australia accomplish little when they act alone; they dig only lowly piles of dirt... As a group, they become builders of immense towers—engineering marvels filled with arches, tunnels, air conditioning systems, and specialized chambers. These intricate towers are the largest structures on earth if you consider the size of their builders. But if we observed only individual termites, we could never predict what they do as a collective. It wouldn't matter how long we observed them as individuals. The skills they have together do not exist in the individuals."

A Simpler Way, by Margaret J. Wheatley and Myron Keller-Rogers

Seeking the Soul of Commerce

Chapter 1

Leonard leaned back in his chair, looked past the file he was holding at the applicant it described, and considered the various polite ways of saying "No."

His office faced west, and through the large window he could see the white peaked mountains that encircled the city. The furnishings were simpler than those of most top executives, almost austere. The most ornate piece was his father's walnut desk, with its carved legs. Nearby, a conference table stood under his trophy wall, where plaques and photos occupied places of honor. Scattered here and there on walls and shelves around the room was a small collection of Iroquois artifacts, including his grandfather's pipe, tobacco pouch, talking stick, and other relics of his people. None of it, with the exception of his desk, had been noticed by the young woman seated in front of him.

Marsha Stone was 22, fresh out of Chelsea University with a certificate in Solid Waste Management, a Bachelor in Environmental Science, and all the other paper credentials the ad had asked for. She'd done all the academic work necessary for a job at the largest company in Chantilly. Marsha looked great on paper, but Leonard wasn't going to hire her, and he couldn't quite explain why, until he remembered Jennifer.

He glanced toward the wall where many of his favorite pictures hung, and sought out the frame around a child's note. Jennifer Henson had first visited the plant on a field trip ten years before, and sent him the note afterward. She returned for an internship during high school, and spent a couple of summers working at Terra, one in the plant and another in shipping, and had gone on to obtain the same certificate and degree as Marsha. The academic work was the same, but Jennifer had acquired experience and an impressive list of references.

As he compared the two young women, he had a vague feeling that the key to Terra's current problems was somewhere in that field trip.

When Leonard first took over as CEO of Terra Waste Management, he focused day and night on meeting the tremendous challenges facing him. But nothing—not his experience, not his leadership skills or education—nothing had prepared him for what lay ahead. The first hints were so subtle, he completely missed them.

The hints came during his first week at "Terra." The company was having serious financial difficulties, but Leonard loved challenges, especially this one—since it touched the past and the future at the same time.

He had tremendous confidence in his abilities, and uprooted his family and relocated to Chantilly without hesitation. He and Alice immediately fell in love with the town and countryside. It was a perfect change for them and, they hoped, for their son.

During that first week, Leonard began to appreciate the truly enormous effort it would take to turn Terra around. Undaunted, on his second Monday as CEO he dropped by the office of the company's most respected researcher, George Aguilera, to ask a few questions.

As Leonard leaned into the opened door of George's office, he was quite startled to see George seated at his small conference table surrounded by schoolchildren. They were talking animatedly, had notebooks open in front of them, and looked like a munchkin board meeting. Leonard felt a twinge of annoyance at the unexpected encounter, spiced with amusement at their appearance. George caught his eye before he could turn away, and called out, "Leonard! Well hello. Come in. Come in. I want you to meet some very special visitors."

The children looked up to see a large man with

Chapter 1

Olympian self-confidence, but little experience in leading children—despite having one of his own.

George made a sweeping gesture toward his guests and said, "These youngsters are on a field trip, part of a class project at Madison Elementary School. They're going to report on what we do here at Terra."

George turned back to the students and said, "You've been planning this report for a long time, haven't you?"

The children nodded their heads—some enthusiastically, while staring straight at Leonard, others shyly, while staring down at the table.

Speaking with the flair of a circus ringleader, George said, "Kids, this is Mr. Leonard Allegren, our new CEO. He's started just this ..."

"What's a CEO?" interrupted a little blonde boy, who'd obviously dressed for an office environment—in a plaid short-sleeve shirt with a bright blue clip-on tie.

George glanced up at Leonard, smiling mischievously and asked, "Do you want to field that one, Mr. Allegren?"

Beginning to respond to George's enthusiasm, Leonard grinned and replied, "No... I suspect you can answer it just fine."

George grinned back and said, "OK, sure."

Leonard was becoming intrigued at how unflustered George was at entertaining a group of school kids. He seemed to delight in Leonard's unexpected appearance. Leonard began to realize that George was a very likeable fellow, as well as an excellent researcher. Rather than retreating, he decided to put his mission on hold for a few minutes and join the fun. He grabbed an empty chair, pulled it up, and sat at the table, hands folded in front of him and eyes staring at George in anticipation.

Seeing that the new arrival was the only one at the table without a notebook, Jenny, the little girl to Leonard's right, slid a sheet of paper over to him.

Meanwhile, focusing on the plaid-shirted boy, George gently said, "Well, Marcus, CEO stands for Chief Executive Officer. The CEO of a company is the person who ..."

"It's like an Indian chief," announced a brunette in a lavender dress seated next to Marcus. She turned to Marcus and added, "Don't you know about chiefs, Marcus? Everybody knows about chiefs!"

George said, "Well, Marsha, a CEO is not exactly ..."

Marcus snapped, "I do too know about chiefs. I know plenty." Marsha had taunted Marcus often before, for the usual reasons, but Marcus wasn't going to tolerate it today. Not with adults around. Leonard lowered his head to hide his suppressed laughter.

"Now, hold on!" George commanded, flashing the palm of his hand like a stop sign. "Let me explain what a Chief Executive Officer is."

"We need to know what they do, too," said a little girl with thick glasses. "Miss Jordan said we should write down what people do, just like they say it."

George straightened, raised both hands palm out, and stared at the children over the top of his glasses like a stern old professor surveying his class. The conference table grew silent as he stared at them, one by one.

Finally, George asked, "Now, what are you doing that isn't working, and what do we need to do to get things done?"

One of the boys replied, "Stop interrupting?"

George nodded and said, "That's right, Ron, and what do you do instead?"

"Raise our hands?"

"Yes Marsha, that's right," said George, "and wait to be recognized. But why is raising your hands the thing to do?"

Chapter 1

Marcus raised his hand, and, when George nodded at him, said, "Because if you can't answer, we can't do our report."

"And?" demanded George.

The children stared at the table, puzzled and bewildered, until George said, "And because if you interrupt someone, you not only stop them from saying what they have to say, but you stop them from contributing to the group. Does everyone understand that? Don't interrupt; raise your hand, and wait. OK?

The children nodded their heads, and George continued.

George grinned playfully, stared straight across the table at Leonard and said, "OK then, listen up, because I'm sure that you'll all find this interesting and useful."

"CEO remember, stands for Chief Executive Officer, and a CEO is like Dr. Edra Brode, the Superintendent of our school system."

Marsha waved her hand and asked, "Who's he?"

"Dr. Brode is your Principal, Mrs. Cunningham's boss."

"Our principal has a boss?" asked Jenny.

Leonard replied, "Yes. Marsha?"

"Dr. Brode tells Mrs. Cunningham what to do?"

Leonard replied, "Not exactly. You know that there is more than one school in Chantilly?"

Jenny's eyes sparkled behind her glasses, as she said, "Oh, yeah, there's lots of schools."

"Well," replied Leonard, "Dr. Brode's job is to think about how all those schools can best help everyone in those schools. Her job is to keep in mind the vision of what you need to be able to do when you finish school, and what you need to learn to be able to do that."

"Mrs Cunningham's job is to make everything go right at your school every day. Do all of you have a pretty good idea of all the things that Mrs. Cunningham does? Marsha?"

"She's very important, that's for sure. Mrs. Cunningham knows a lot, and she tells all the teachers what to do. She told me I always look very nice."

"Very good." said George. "Marcus?"

"When I was little, she told me not to run in the halls, because I could hurt myself or somebody else. So, I don't run anymore."

"Very good. Jenny?"

Jenny lowered her hand to her glasses, pushed them more firmly onto her nose and said, "When we have assemblies, Mrs. Cunningham always talks on the microphone first, and tells us about things. She's in charge of everything."

George nodded and said, "Well now, there you go, Jenny. She's in charge of things. So, tell me, all of you, what do you think you have to do when you're in charge of things? What kind of work do you do when you're in charge? Marcus?"

Marcus waited until everyone had turned to look at him and said, "You've got to make people do what you say or else! You have to let people know that you're the boss."

"Ron?"

"Yeah, and when people are bad, they have to go to your office and you call their mom." Ron grinned at the memory and said, "Like lat week when one of the boys started a fight. Mrs. Cunningham called his mom, and boy was he in trouble." Then he frowned and asked, "Who does a CEO call when people are bad?"

"Hah! Good question." George noted with a hearty laugh. "So, who will you be calling, do you think, Mr. Allegren?"

Leonard gave George a mock look of disapproval, and then shrugged good-naturedly.

"Actually," George continued, "the CEO of a company like Terra is like Mrs. Cunningham in some ways, but there's an important difference. Everyone in our company is all grown up and is expected to act like a grown up. As adults, the people who work here are responsible for their own behavior. So, as our new CEO, Mr. Allegren is here to help us do our jobs better. He sees all the parts of the company and all the people in it, and he's here to make sure everything and everybody works well together. It's a lot like what goes on in your own homes. You know how your Mom and Dad make sure that everything goes the way it should—that you have good food and eat when you should, you make it to school on time, and that the house is clean, the yard mowed, and all that good stuff? But as you get older and start growing up, you help them out more and more, right? You begin doing things for yourself without being told, and your Mom and Dad begin to depend on you to do things to help keep everything going."

A hand shot up, waved excitedly and George said, "Yes, Marcus?"

"I do that! My mom and dad call me their 'trash man' cause I take the trash out every Tuesday right after school. I always do it, unless I'm really sick or something. Always."

"Marsha?"

"You know what I do? I unload the dishwasher when Mom is making dinner. And I set the table. I'm really, really good at it, too. Everybody says so."

"Ron?"

Squirming in his seat while he spoke, Ron said, "I take care of Roger, our dog. I have to feed him his food and keep his water dish filled. He's really big, and he drinks lots and lots of water. Gulp, gulp, gulp, with his big tongue. And he gets it all over the floor and I have to wipe it up. Whewee. What a messy dog! I help Dad give him a bath, too, because he's too big for me to hang onto by myself. Boy, he doesn't like that. He always gets us all wet, and I have to put on a new shirt when we're all done."

George leaned over the table toward the kids, looking at them very intensely and said, "Now all that stuff's a lot of work, but it sure makes you feel good, doesn't it? It's really important, and when you do really important things, it makes you feel really good, right?"

All of the children nodded enthusiastically.

George sat up straight and crossed his arms. "You know," he said, "if I had to say what the most important thing that a CEO does in a company, guess what it would be? A CEO is always reminding people how important their work is, and how important they are for doing it. When you forget how important your work is you sometimes don't do it as well as you should—like forgetting to take out the trash, letting Roger run out of water, or... Marsha?"

"Or putting dishes away wet, into the cupboard. I never do that."

"Right! That's it. Absolutely right." George peeked over at Leonard. Leonard laughed and pointed to the sheet of paper lying before him on the table.

Leonard said, "I got it all down, George, just like you said it."

Leonard was amazed at George's chutzpah in declaring his philosophy of good leadership in front of his new boss, highly amused, but not the least bit annoyed. He found George's style and lecturette highly reassuring. But, at the same time, as the enormous obstacles to saving Terra Waste Management rushed back into his consciousness, he thought, *"If it were only that simple."*

Leonard enjoyed his time with the school kids, but was anxious to get on with his agenda for the day. He'd risen from his chair and was about to bid the kids a gra-

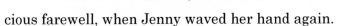

cious farewell, when Jenny waved her hand again.

"Yes Jenny?" asked George.

"I have a question for Mr. Allegren."

Leonard paused and asked, "Yes?"

"How did you get to know everything so you could become the boss? Did you go to school to find out everything before you came?"

Leonard sat back down, looked over at George with a big grin and said, "It's a good thing that Jenny wasn't heading the Search Committee, isn't it?"

Then he turned to Jenny and said, "Now, that's a pretty tough question. Hmm."

Leonard thought silently for about fifteen seconds as everyone watched him closely, tapping his chin with his right index finger while he composed a reply. Finally, he said, "You know, Jenny, I can't say that I know everything there is to know about Terra. But I do know this much. There are a lot of really smart people here who do special kinds of work and they're experts—they have a very special knowledge—about what they do. Much more knowledge about it than other people have. My job is to think about the future, and make sure we work together to solve problems."

Leonard gestured toward George and said, "Take Mr. Aguilera here. Mr. Aguilera is a scientist. He has a lot more knowledge about the important scientific work that our company does than I do. In fact, that's why I came down here today—to ask him some questions about the work he does so that I can understand it better. Yes, Marcus?"

"Why do you have to understand it better, Mr. Allegren? Why don't you just let him do his work and leave him alone? Nobody asks me about how I take the trash out anymore. I know how to do it, and I like to just do it without being bothered. Carrie, my little sister, sometimes bothers me when I'm doing it, but she doesn't count."

Leonard nodded his head and replied, "Well, Marcus, that's a really good question. But let me tell you something that I hope you'll all remember. We never do anything perfectly. We may think that we're doing it the best way it could be done, but there's almost always some way to do it even better. Now, I have no doubt that you're really good at taking out the trash, but I bet that you could do it even a little bit better."

Leonard held his right hand out in front of him with his thumb and index finger pressed tightly against each other to demonstrate just how small such improvements can be and said, "There's always room for improvement, even if it's just a tiny bit. Sometimes it really helps to talk to somebody else about what you're doing because... well, maybe together you will discover a way to do it even better. You should never be afraid to ask questions about how you could do something better, or find someone to help you ask the questions."

Most of the children cast wide-eyed gazes toward Leonard, while a couple frowned of confusion. Finally, Marsha raised her hand and objected, "I empty the dishwasher the very best that it can be. I can tell you that for certain. Ask my Mom if you don't believe it."

Leonard smiled and said, "I'm sure you do, Marsha, but maybe if something were changed, something you can't do yourself, to the sink or the soap or something, there might be a way to do it even better."

Marsha reacted to this idea with a huff, folded her arms over her chest, and slumped back in her chair. Leonard had encountered many people who were unreceptive to new ideas, if seldom so young, and recognized that further argument was useless.

George jumped in and said, "I have to say that it's been my experience that Mr. Allegren is right. That's what we scientists are always doing. We're always trying to find out more, to understand things better, so we can find a better way—or even an entirely new way—of doing things. That's what makes my job so fun—knowing that there's the chance you'll discover something new about the world, and that maybe that discovery will lead to a better way of doing things and of helping people."

Leonard smiled at George, nodded and said, "Well, I'll tell you what. Why don't you just think about what I've said? You might make some discoveries. In the meantime, I'd better get back to work. I have a lot of questions to ask. But I've really enjoyed meeting all of you."

Leonard shook every child's hand, even Marsha's, and their faces beamed with delight at the attention.

"Well, so long for now," said Leonard. "I need to borrow Mr. Aguilera for a couple of moments, but I'll send him right back."

Both men walked to the door of George's office and huddled for a second with their backs to the conference table.

"Well, George," Leonard whispered, "what's going on?"

George replied, "I know we've a lot to talk about, and I really want to get to it, but I didn't want to disappoint these kids. Their teacher called me last week and told me how excited they were about the trip. Besides, it's good community relations. These kinds of activities send messages to kids about the future, you know."

"Of course."

"Give me half an hour and I'll stop by your office, if that's OK."

"That'll be fine, George, but be prepared to spend some time."

Suddenly, Leonard felt something tugging at his

jacket. When he turned around, he discovered Jenny, standing with notepad in hand, looking up at him through her thick lenses. "Jenny?" he asked.

"Mr. Allegren, I still don't understand something I need to know for our report."

"Yes?"

"Why didn't they choose someone who already knows everything, to be boss? I mean, why didn't they get someone who doesn't have to go around asking a lot of questions?"

George stepped in and said, "Unfortunately, Jenny. Mr. Allegren really does have to get back to his job, but I'll talk with you about that after he's gone, OK? I'm sure I can explain it just fine."

George gently directed Jenny back to her table, and Leonard left. As a result, he missed George's explanations of leadership and creativity.

A week later, he received thank you notes from all of them. He smiled at Jenny's, and decided to have it framed and hung on his trophy.

Chapter 2

Today's Students Don't Meet the Mark

"Apollo was the self-appointed bearer of Truth, and he understood the task of interpreting for men the will of his father Zeus. Apollo symbolizes the duality of the Hellenic spirit: the urge to ideals, to truth, to beauty, to spirituality and sacredness, and the accompanying desire to plumb the profane, the ugly, the corrupt, and the fleshly."

David Kiersey

Chapter 2

Leonard never did ask George how he'd answered Jenny's leadership question. He had always been clear about what leadership was to him, hadn't thought much about it from other perspectives, and his efforts to *save* Terra captured his attention and obscured the memory, until now.

Thinking about it now, he realized it was a good question. Despite Terra's success during his tenure, that question, and the suggestion that leaders have ready-made answers, almost haunted him. Leonard knew he'd been a highly effective leader when measured by the metrics. Since his arrival, Terra had emerged from near bankruptcy and been transformed into a highly profitable company well-known for its innovative future waste treatment projects, so respected that the "Engineering Services" division had just been invited to bid on yet another treatment plant in China. Still, tomorrow loomed, and the future felt like the creeping darkness of an early and unexpected sunset. He had always had a passion to do more, to make a difference and leave something better than he found it. This time, the job before him challenged his self-confidence in a way he didn't understand and couldn't name.

"The future just ain't what it used to be," he thought. *"In fact, what is it in me that even makes me believe I can help Terra move into the future?"*

Leonard suspected that George's pending retirement—the fourth of a valued, veteran employee in as many months—was triggering tonight's malaise. But there was more to it. It felt like Terra's energy, its sense of direction, of excitement, was seeping away. Marsha and the other potential hires he'd interviewed recently had the requisite paper credentials, but none of them seemed to have a sense of... of passion... of imagination... of wanting to join something bigger than themselves. So many were focused on the benefits they would be entitled to from the job, from Terra, rather than what value they would bring to the company.

Leonard reflected many times, during countless interviews, whether he was being fair, or whether it was simply a generational thing—the style of kids today—but he didn't think so. He'd given them every opportunity to show their stuff, had asked thoughtful, detailed, open-ended questions. Many of them could recite processes and methodologies well enough. But few of them showed the slightest grasp of the possibilities underlying those processes, or of where their prospective job fit in the big picture of the company. Only the Jennys got it.

The disinterested flatness of the other young hopefuls disturbed him, and he could not, would not, turn Terra over to them. Terra needed energy, imagination, passion, and experience beyond paper credentials.

Leonard had come to love Terra Waste Management precisely because, at its core, there was nothing mediocre about it. When Leonard took the helm, the company had been mismanaged for many years. Its stock had dropped to 40% of its original value. Even though its previous leader was an active, popular figure in the community, for many years investors and employees alike called it, "Terra-ble Waste of Money." Its last breath had been rattling in its throat, and Leonard had reached in and pulled it back to life.

Some of what he'd done hadn't made him popular with the locals, but that wasn't the point. He'd salvaged the dying company that the local economy depended on; and frankly, Leonard didn't mourn the loss of willful incompetence and obstructionism.

What drove Leonard was the surge of vitality and

Chapter 2

excitement that emerged following the excision of those who "just didn't get it," and those who hid in the bureaucracy. The ingenuity and resourcefulness of the remaining staff, from the scientists to the marketing team, were exhilarating. Leonard had become accustomed to working in the midst of it, and much of that excitement and awareness of possibility came from working closely with minds like George's, and now they were leaving, retiring, and he couldn't come close to replacing them.

An era was coming to an end, and it wasn't just the passing of a way of life or the departure of respected colleagues, it was the passing of a way of knowing, of perceiving one's work and purpose. Whatever that perception was, most young applicants didn't have it, and Leonard didn't see how Terra could survive without it.

After sending Marsha on her way, Leonard considered the next item on his agenda, George's retirement celebration. Taking a deep breath, he turned his thoughts to the evening ahead and right away he wondered if that reporter, McKenzie Jordan, would be there. She never seemed to miss an opportunity to write about each Terra retirement as if it was another sign of the last days before the Apocalypse. *"What possible good is there in spewing a constant barrage of bad news,"* Leonard asked himself? He preferred to be left alone to run his business. *"Let the results speak for themselves,"* he thought.

He rubbed his aching eyes. It was late, he was tired, and, looking at the clock on his desk, he realized he had to leave the office now if he was going to arrive on time.

He reached inside his suit jacket to make sure he had the notes for his speech, and then left the building.

As he neared his Jag, Millie, Leonard pressed the button on his keychain, unlocking the driver's door and turning off the alarm. The soft, sleek, leather seat enfolded him, and vague feelings of dissatisfaction prepared to surface. But a memory thrust those feelings aside, and he recalled something his dad used to say to his own employees, "People supply the vision, science supplies the tools, and together we build the future." It fit George, one of the most innovative, creative, and imaginative men he had ever known, and Leonard realized that nothing in his notes adequately described the real story of what George had meant to Terra, and to him.

As he drove Millie out the gate, and sped off, he realized that, for the first time, he doubted that Terra could find the answers within itself. His management team didn't have the answers he needed, they were somewhere else, and he didn't know where or how to find them.

Chapter 3

Getting Ready to Ask Hard Questions

You've seen a herd of goats
going down to the water.
The lame and dreamy goat
brings up the rear.
There are worried faces about that one,
but now they're laughing,
because look, as they return,
that goat is leading!
There are many different kinds of knowing.
The lame goat's kind is a branch
that traces back to the root of presence.
Learn from the lame goat,
and lead the herd home.

Rumi

Seeking the Soul of Commerce

Chapter 3

McKenzie Jordan crumpled the ripped pantyhose, tossed them to the floor as if they were part of a conspiracy, and stared scornfully at the ruined heap. It had been one of her "bad" days, as emotional swells rushed from highs to lows. Fortunately, she'd been able to spend most of the day at home, finishing some personal research in her beloved map room, but now it was time to get ready for a party she had mixed feelings about. She didn't have any patience for pantyhose with runs.

George Aguilera's retirement party was this evening, and she had to cover it for both KCCT and the Chantilly Chronicle. But, like so many others in Chantilly, she had a deep love and respect for George and would never have missed his party.

Her roles as personal friend, reporter, and local feature news broadcaster made this event awkward, and she wished she could just relax and enjoy herself. Claiming victory over the impudent nylons, she reached for them with a swift swoop and pitched them into the trash. "Tonight, I shall be free of any obstructions or limitations," she declared to herself as she wriggled into her longest black skirt, hiding all that might have been viewed by a casual observer, grabbed her purse and an almost new dress bag, stepped into her tiny kitchen, and poured a cup of coffee. Repeating the comforting ritual learned from her journalism mentor, she set the purse on the little table in her breakfast nook, sat down, and began going through it. First out was her pen and pocket notebook, with a checklist of reminders on who she needed to see tonight, and what she should ask them about their relationship to George. Then, her micro recorder, with extra batteries and memory cards, her wallet and lipstick du jour. She placed them all carefully inside the dress bag, which she used so seldom it still had a price tag on the inside. But tonight was special, so she was careful to discard change and crumpled handkerchiefs, and placed only what she needed inside this special bag. With the tools of her trade accounted for, she sat back, closed her eyes, and imagined a perfect evening.

An enormous feeling of warmth toward George surged up, and her eyes began to water. She and George went back a long way. As a very young woman—teaching journalism at Chantilly High—she had had quite a crush on him. Of course, any romantic notions were overridden by the fact that George was a very happily married older man. But her genuine affection for him had not diminished. There was something about George that conjured hope and unparalleled optimism in those around him.

However, his boss... Well, the very thought of Leonard evoked a maddening frustration, and she hoped his likely presence at the party—his aloof, Olympian speech—would not ruin it.

She tensed at the thought, and began heart breathing like George had taught her—into the heart, and out, into the heart, and out—until she had calmed down. Then she walked back into her room to finish fixing her hair.

When she finally stepped out of her front door, McKenzie looked and felt remarkably elegant, despite the day's emotional turmoil. A magnificent sunset was a very pleasant surprise, and she paused to admire the blazing golds and yellows that cast fire on the green slopes of the mountains to the west of Chantilly.

"My God, how beautiful!" she whispered. She pulled

on her front door until she could hear it lock, walked to the porch swing and sat briefly as she admired the sight. She breathed some more—cleansing breaths to breathe in the light and breathe out the toxic emotions. As she breathed, her face settled into a restful peace. She knew that, sitting alone on her porch, she was feeling the same reverence that millions of humans had experienced over the ages.

Finally, McKenzie realized she was going to be late if she didn't leave, and headed for her aging Honda Civic.

When the front door opened, Dusty shouted, "Mommy!" leaped up, and ran out of the room. George and Donna, smiling in anticipation, and helped each other rise from the floor of the den where they'd been playing with their grandson. Moments later, their daughter Elizabeth walked in, with Dusty gripping her left hand. Elizabeth hugged each of her parents with a single squeeze of her right arm; grinning at sight of the only couple she knew who had been together for more than ten years.

Elizabeth asked, "Are you sure this is OK?"

George replied, "It's only a couple hours a day after school. We love taking care of him, and now that I'm retired, I have the time. Besides, having him around has helped me in my job at the University."

"How's that, Daddy?"

"Well, I can't go into much of it now, but, one of the graduate classes I'll be starting after this week will be looking at workforce issues for the future, Dusty's future! So, I'm trying to get a better understanding about what youngsters need in order to be prepared for the future. Our Terra H.R. folks have been growing increasingly distraught over the quality of new applicants, so

I'm going to have my business graduate students have a look at the issue for Leonard."

"Oh Daddy, when I was little you taught me to ask questions about everything and it made me so mad because I never could just accept what was going on like every one else. It made my life so hard," she joked.

"Yes," said Donna with a smile, it's clear you've suffered a lot."

George picked up Donna's coat from the back of a chair, as Donna reminded George, "The retirement's not official until the party is over."

George helped Donna into her coat and asked, "Are you ready?"

Donna replied, "Always, with you."

Chapter 4

Assimilating Relevant Data

"The universe exists in order that the experiencer
may experience it, and thus become liberated."
How to Know God, the Aphorisms of Pantanjali

Seeking the Soul of Commerce

Chapter 4

The Chantilly Community Center was hopping to the beat of a 50s revival band, crooning favorites from George's youth. Dozens of dancers guided each other around the center of the main hall. An enormous quilt—months in the making—hung from the ceiling over the band, declared, "We Love You George!" in vibrant colors.

Leonard had little interest in parties of any kind. Of course, he and Alice attended the obligatory industry dinners and award functions, with all the good humor those occasions required. The number of invitations grew following Terra's recovery, but he preferred riding his trail bike or catching up on his business reading. Still, over the years he had attended many goodbye parties, mostly brief gatherings around store-bought cake in corporate conference rooms. Those occasions barely interrupted the work day and blended together in everyone's memory. But this time, George's fellow employees had insisted on organizing something special for him, and they'd turned it into an *event* that would make the first page of the next day's Chronicle.

The dining tables circling the hall were graced by beds of flowers, lit by candles, and covered by elegant tablecloths—obviously whisked for the evening from linen cabinets throughout Chantilly. At each table were china place settings for six, again—judging from the variety of patterns and styles—borrowed from china cabinets and kitchen cupboards for a special celebration.

Yet more astounding were the buffet tables strategically placed throughout the hall. Obviously someone—Leonard suspected his production manager—had carefully planned the best layout to avoid long, cumbersome, lines. Each table glowed with candlelight from thoughtfully situated candelabras, and the smells that emanated from those tables were beyond words. The best cuisine every home could offer, the culinary specialty of every household, was on display waiting to be sampled. It was all astoundingly lush and personal. There wasn't a catered dish anywhere.

Hundreds of streamers draped across the large ceiling enhanced the festive display, and the walls were festooned with collages of snapshots and home-sewn banners.

Leonard scanned the magical hall and the bustling crowd in amazement at the display, and with pride in his coworkers. They'd done all this for George, right under his nose *"Talk about project management!"*

His delight and amazement plunged into to mild annoyance when he spotted McKenzie Jordan amidst a group of senior employees. A powerful presence in both local television and the newspaper, she'd been building up her career with aggressive reporting, dogging every action at Terra, making negative allusions to Leonard's leadership skills and stopping just shy of calling him incompetent.

McKenzie's attire was less festive than he might have expected for a party, but it flattered her magnificent hair and showed off her admirable figure. Leonard assumed she was at the party to dig up more spurious dirt, and was dressed to encourage indiscretions and to look good for the news cameras.

Ordinarily he'd have stayed out of her way, but instead, he hid his true feelings behind a smile and ignored her. Unfortunately, McKenzie spotted him from across the hall, broke off her conversation, and strode toward him.

Leonard turned away from her to a nearby buffet and grabbed a cup and a plate. When he turned back, he found McKenzie nearing him, and greeted her with a forced smile and a shallow nod.

Chapter 4

McKenzie smiled disarmingly and asked, "Well, Mr. Allegren, what do you think of the party?"

"It's magnificent! His friends have really outdone themselves. It's what they wanted and no one could have done it better."

McKenzie swept her hand across the panorama of candle lit tables, buffets and mementos and said, "I'm glad the camera crew and photographer are here. I don't think anything I could say would do it justice. It's a remarkable display of respect... and ... and real affection."

"Yes, it is."

"It must be very hard to lose George."

"To lose him? No... not to lose him, he's earned this retirement of his, if you can call it that."

"You're referring to his new teaching job?" asked McKenzie.

"Associate Professor at Chelsea University; he's always loved teaching kids, and they love him. He's been our best recruiter. I couldn't tell you how many of the children he's helped over the years have come back to us as young adults, hoping for a position at Terra."

"I know. I'm doing a piece on him."

"Oh? For your column?"

"On him, for the column, and as part of an upcoming story for the station."

"And you're poking around now, at his party?"

McKenzie's voice rose slightly, as she said, "He's my friend too, Mr. Allegren. I'm not 'poking around.'" Pointing at a collage near the entrance, she said, "Some of those photos are mine. But nothing interferes with my reporting. Nothing."

"That almost sounds like a motto, Ms. Jordan."

"I suppose it is."

"Well, I admire your persistence, if not your perspective. But if you will excuse me, I haven't eaten since lunch—"

Just then, the band began playing Roy Orbison's *Pretty Woman*. Startled by the change, Leonard glanced toward the stage and spotted George next to the band leader.

McKenzie said, "Mr. Allegren, we really do need to talk."

"Oh?" Leonard replied, cocking his left eyebrow upward. "Is it something Marci can help you with?"

"No, I've had enough encounters with your Community Relations Department. I need to talk with you. Really talk."

Leonard spotted the Chronicle's photographer focusing on the dancers, grinned roguishly and said, "Well, how about now? Do you dance?"

"What?"

"Want to talk? Then come on." Leonard put down his plate and cup, and strode out onto the floor, coaxing her in the general direction of the photographer. Once they reached a clear spot, visible to the camera and free of dancers, he turned and offered her his hand. She took it reluctantly, and allowed him to guide her around the floor.

"Now, what did you want to talk about, Ms. Jordan?"

A flash went off, and McKenzie realized that their location, near the photographer, was no accident. She hoped her editor wouldn't choose one of *these* photos!

"Um... I have some important things to share... that you need to know."

"Oh? And just what could we have to talk about?"

"Mr. Allegren, Leonard, I wouldn't be putting myself through this..."

Another brilliant flash, and McKenzie silently cursed the photographer.

"Embarrassment?" added Leonard.

Chapter 4

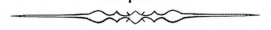

"...if it wasn't important," continued McKenzie, "but this isn't the—"

Leonard spun McKenzie outward, in time to the music, held her there for a beat, then reeled her back into his arms.

"But here we are, McKenzie. If you want to talk, this is the time and the place."

"No, Leonard, I'm not embarrassed. I'm proud of my work, of getting at and writing about the *truth*. I've been watching Terra Waste Management for years. This isn't the first retirement party I've attended, and I know you're losing, have already lost, a lot of your key people. You haven't replaced most of them, and I want to know what you're doing about it! Terra is the biggest employer in Chantilly. The whole regional economy depends on it, and the community deserves to know what's going on."

"And so you want what, a heart-to-heart on our staffing problems, so you can televise another expose? I'm running a business, McKenzie, not managing your career."

"Is that how you see me, a nosy reporter digging for a story? How would you know what I am? You've never come down off your mountain enough to talk with me before, with anyone. What do you know about this community, about our lives? Leonard, you're a leader, the one responsible for holding the vision of Terra. But you can't do that properly if you don't understand people's lives. It's time you..."

"Their lives are their own concern, McKenzie, not mine."

The music ended, the dancers stilled and, except for Leonard and McKenzie, began clapping.

"It's time to end this dance, and our conversation," Leonard announced, his face flushed, "My wife has arrived, and I must do what I came here to do, celebrate the retirement of one of my finest employees and *my friend.* Now, if you will excuse me."

McKenzie straightened, stared straight into his eyes and said, "Leonard, you can't afford to brush me off. You're wrong about my intentions, you really are, and you can't afford to be wrong this time."

Leonard had begun to turn away, but was halted by the sincerity in her voice.

Sensing his hesitation, McKenzie smiled and asked, "So, shall we continue this later, Leonard?"

Leonard nodded, said, "You know my number," and then completed his turn and walked toward his wife.

As McKenzie watched Leonard leave, she felt a momentary rush of compassion for him, almost protectiveness. But, she dismissed it and dove back into the party. She had work to do.

Donna watched from her table until Leonard was far enough away from McKenzie, and then waved her over to her side of the room where she met her part way. They hugged as close friends and McKenzie asked, "Well, how's it feel to have George home full time?"

Donna smiled and said, "It's wonderful, but he's keeping busy. He's teaching night classes at the college, and taking care of Dusty after school.

"How's Isabel?"

McKenzie replied, "Great. She's been accepted at Chelsea University, and we're just waiting for the student visa to go through."

Donna said, "Wow, congratulations! Are you sure you're ready to go from living alone to having a teenager in the house?"

McKenzie smiled ruefully and replied, "Is anyone? I've been preparing, and I have friends I hope will help.

Chapter 4

Besides, she seems much more... serious, focused, than most American kids."

Donna said, "George was that way when he came to the United States, too."

McKenzie replied, "That's right, they're both from Costa Rica."

Donna said, "Yes, but he's from the city, and she's a village girl.

"But listen... Remember the article you wrote a couple weeks ago on the problems businesses are having with medical costs and retirement benefits spiraling out of control? I wondered if you learned anything about my company while researching it?"

McKenzie replied, "Mega Pixels? Why?"

Donna glanced around, lowered her voice and said, "Well, there are some rumors going around at work, about layoffs, outsourcing, that sort of thing, and I can't piece it together. They're having problems, but they won't say how bad it is and what they're doing about it, and I wondered if, when you did that medical care and benefits article, if you heard anything about this."

McKenzie frowned in sympathy and said, "About *your* company? You're what, eighteen months from retirement?"

"Seventeen," replied Donna.

McKenzie said, "I haven't heard anything, but I'll check into it and let you know if I come across anything," then turned toward a sound at the podium.

Seeking the Soul of Commerce

Chapter 5

Using Inspiration to Communicate
and Interact With Others

Although the balance sheet lists the value of the physical assets, the true value of a business is measured by the quality and diversity of its people and their relationships.

Seeking the Soul of Commerce

Chapter 5

The battered podium—veteran of generations of community luncheons—was doing its best to hold both Leonard's notes and his weight as he leaned casually, and perhaps overconfidently, against it. He was widely acknowledged as an enthusiastic and inspiring speaker, and projected a powerful personal presence, when the occasion demanded.

The crowd quieted as everyone noticed his presence, and made their way to their chairs. Without speaking a word he moved his gaze from his notes to the table where George and their wives were seated, to the decorations around the hall and the faces of the crowd. And at that point, Leonard realized that all of it confirmed his earlier thought that his prepared speech was wholly inadequate to the man he... they... were celebrating.

Smiling, he snatched up the sheets of paper, crumpled them into a ball, and tossed them over his shoulder with an overacted casualness. A soft chuckle rumbled through the crowd and Leonard said, "Everything I was going to say—praise for his achievements, his role in saving Terra Waste Management, his contributions to the science of Waste Recovery and Recycling—merely echoes *what* we all know he's *done*. And that's not why we're here. We're all here because of *who* George *is*, to each of us and to all of us, because of the influence he's had in our lives, on *who we are* now because of him. I don't really know what to say, or how to say it, but after seeing this hall tonight, I'm certain you all do. So, I'm going to ask all of you to join me in sharing with George what he has meant to you.

"For myself, George, working with you has been one of the most rewarding professional and personal experiences of my whole life." Leonard tapped his chest with his right hand, and then waved his hand expansively over the crowd, as he said, "And I *know* that *all of you* feel the same.

At their table, George took his wife, Donna's, hand in his and cradled it, and her eyes began to tear. Leonard's wife took Donna's other hand and held it as Leonard continued.

"We've been through the fire of recovery and the complacency of success, and always George was there with his wise and focused counsel. It was George, in fact, who taught me that while great scientists are not always great leaders, great leaders are always great scientists, great creative thinkers. The first time I ran into George at Terra he was handling a crew of youngsters who were full of curiosity and questions about our work. For them, everything was possible if only they asked the right questions. His patience and delight at every question was incredible. Later he explained to me that he loved working with young people because they were the most natural scientists of all. It is us, the adults in their lives, who drum out their enthusiasm because we tell them it is hard, or we become afraid, tired or embarrassed about not knowing all the answers. All too often, we don't know how to help them, or how to get help for them.

'Being a good scientist isn't about having the right answers,' he would tell me, 'it is about asking the right questions, and being passionate about finding the answers.' One day, when I was struggling with a tough issue, he came into my office, and as my finest counselor and my very good friend, his response to my dilemma was simple, 'Leonard,' he said, 'the decision you will have to make will take great courage. You will have to question everything that has ever been done in the past. You will have to think differently and you will have to get others to do the same. But to do any less will not be a display of cowardice. You see, the opposite of courage is not cowardice; it is conformity, the most egregious failure of leader. A good leader takes people where they want to go, where it is comfortable, and familiar. A great leader takes people where they need to go.' On the way over here tonight I wavered, George. For a moment, thinking about not having your counsel available to me every day, I forgot that I am a scientist too. I know how to ask questions, and together with Terra's team we'll always find the right answers. I will miss your daily presence, George, but I will never fail to seek your friendly counsel." For a moment, silence engulfed them all.

"Now, who else would like to share?"

Dozens of hands shot up. Leonard waved them to the steps leading to the stage, organized them into a long line, and shepherded them to the battered podium. Schoolchildren, parents, collegians, former fellow employees, and elderly retirees, all poured out their words of heartfelt appreciation for someone they all considered a great leader and a personal friend.

Despite all of his well-known thoughtfulness and wisdom, George was unprepared for this abundance, and soon his tears joined Donna's.

The praise continued for forty-three minutes, with Leonard steering each person to the microphone, encouraging them to say what was in their hearts. When everyone was done, Leonard led them in a standing ovation, and amidst the thunderous applause, waved George up to the stage.

After a last hand squeeze from Donna, George stood and waded through the crowd. The thunderous applause washed over him. Men patted him on the back, gripped a shoulder, shook a hand. Women kissed and hugged him. When George reached the podium, he raised his hands to quiet the crowd, and then Leonard handed him the mike.

Beaming, George took the mike, swallowed and said, "I can't believe you've done all this," waving his arm to encompass the whole, wonderful, scene. "Donna and I will remember this moment for the rest of our lives, it's overwhelming."

The crowd gazed at George in a beautiful silence, as he continued, "

"'Retire' is a funny word; sort of feels like bedtime has arrived and you're supposed to put all your toys away, brush your teeth, turn out the lights and jump into the sack—so Daddy and Mommy can finally relax. When I was a kid, that idea—disappearing so everybody else could have fun—didn't appeal to me, and it still doesn't. Donna and I will be here for many years, continuing to make our contribution to the community. And in a sense, what we've done up to now has led up to what we can do going forward.

"Donna and I have always been a team. When I was offered my first position with Terra, those many years ago, Donna did not understand how I could consider making a career out of *trash*. She did not understand what I found attractive about *waste*. She was, quite properly, concerned about how she would explain my work to our friends, and how our son would explain it to his classmates."

As George spoke, McKenzie was standing next to an old schoolmate, Sandra Benton, who leaned over and said, "God, I love George. I'm going to miss having him around."

McKenzie turned and said, "Me too." in Sandra's ear.

"Funny thing is," Sandra said, "I never worked that closely with George. The research lab could be the

Chapter 5

planet Pluto as far as I am concerned. But Dr. Terra—that's what we all call him—somehow you just keep running into him."

Sandra turned away and joined in the applause as George handed the microphone back to Leonard. Just then, a high-pitched screech blasted the room. When it had faded away, Leonard said, "Sorry about that." and another feedback squeal blasted from the speakers. One of the tech guys from Terra leaped onto the side of the stage and dashed into the back to fiddle with the amplifier.

Leonard paused, gazing into the wing to his left, said, "Testing... testing... testing," until he got a high sign. Then, he turned to George and said, "I hope you realize, George, that we're not letting you out of here without a good old-fashioned retirement speech. We want a real speech, don't we?" Leonard asked, turning back around to the audience.

The crowd began chanting, "Speech. Speech. Speech." and began stomping their feet to the beat. George grinned sheepishly. Leonard waved the crowd to silence, handed George the microphone, and walked off-stage to his left.

George stood before them for a few moments and then said, "There's so much I need to tell you that I've had difficulty imagining where to start. But, Donna and I talked it over, and I'm just going to let my heart take me where it wants to go. ...

"The world would classify me as a man of science ... and in some respects I am. But I've always preferred to integrate things, rather than to separate and classify them. In fact, one of the things I've always loved about science is its ability to show us how everything is related, and I've come to realize that I love science because I love life. They're both full of endless surprises. You can never know what's around the corner. And you learn to respect, to revere, both science and life, because they insist on being just what they are.

"So, I didn't become a scientist so that I could collect knowledge and solve problems. That was a part of it, yes, but not the part that grabbed me and made me love it. No, what I've always loved, what I couldn't resist, was the adventure—the adventure of plunging into the unknown without knowing where it's going to take you. And, as Leonard just said, asking questions. In a way, I'm an adrenaline junky who hangs out in the science lab."

George straightened, and glared out at the audience.

"And that brings me to Terra Waste Management. If we spent our days, months, and years in Terra just running around managing waste, you wouldn't be here celebrating Donna and me. I'd have packed up and moved on decades ago!

"Think about it. When I came here I had a fine career in Energy Science. Why would I get involved in garbage? Why would I move into what everyone thought was an industry with no future and no career prospects?

"I came to Terra for the adventure. Oh, like everyone today, Terra manages everything—time, stress, change, ambiguity. We manage, manage, manage.

"But that isn't real; it's not what makes a company work, or keeps it working, and it's not what made Terra profitable."

George leaned toward the hall full of friends and associates and declared, "The reality is that at Terra, we've never been in the business of *managing* waste. We've always been in the business of *exploring* waste—of discovering what it really is and what it's good for. Again, asking questions.

"My mother was a gardener, all her life, and I remember one spring day when she was out weeding. It was a fine sunny morning, just before siesta. I asked her

Chapter 5

what a weed was. She told me a weed was either a plant whose purpose we knew, but which was growing in the wrong place, or it was a plant whose purpose we didn't know.

"Decades ago when my mom asked me why I took this job, I reminded her of that spring morning, and told her that waste is a lot like that. It's just stuff whose purpose we don't know, or that's in the wrong place. And our job at Terra is discovering what the purpose of that stuff or resource is, and returning it to the right place.

"Mom was always proud of my work after that, and I've tried to help all of you be proud too.

"And we should be proud. We're in the business of discovering the purpose and use of these abundant resources. Over the past two decades we've helped redefine the whole concept of waste. We've discovered the possibilities *for* life in things others flushed away or dismissed as a drain on life.

"And all of you know how we did it, each of us here, in our own way. We did it through exploration and adventure. We looked this huge ugly monster in the face, and we kept on looking until we could see what we had not been able to see before. Then, inch by inch, chemical by chemical, molecule by molecule, question by question, we transformed it!"

The hall broke out in applause again. George waited patiently for a few moments and then raised his left hand for silence.

"Many people view science as a mass of horrible technicalities. We've all seen that reaction. But how did that happen? How did science become so alien to so many people? This is a great puzzle to me, because in my universe we're all scientists. We're all adventurers. Science emerged from the core of the human soul, from our spiritual craving to understand. Thus, science is not just an occupational or business specialty. It's not technology, laboratories, or research institutes. Science is a *way of being*, a way of viewing and experiencing life. And as a way of being, it belongs to all of us, and it's part of who we are.

"As I gaze around this room, I see embodied in you the secret behind great science and great adventure."

George began pacing back and forth across the stage, totally absorbed in his words.

Leonard had settled into a relaxed-tension, in anticipation of one of George's revelations.

McKenzie had been captivated by the building intensity and held motionless, waiting for it to break.

Suddenly, George stopped pacing and turned to face the crowd.

"Yes, looking out at this room, I see... I feel... I know what it takes to make great things happen."

George nodded his head thoughtfully, affirming the rightness of his insight.

"I know exactly what it is that makes things happen."

George threw a pointed finger out at the audience and yelled, "Right here! Right now. Within you," jabbing his finger forward, "and within me." jabbing it at his own chest. "We are the force—us together—that make things happen. The creativity that makes new things come to life isn't in the tools we use, it's in *us*. Problems are solved right here.

"We used to know that, when we were young. While our conscious minds have forgotten, some part of us, deep within, still remembers.

"Years ago I was watching a PBS series by Bill Moyers on poets and poetry in America. It was terrific! And I remember—and will never forget—a young woman he featured on the show named Naomi Nye. She told the story that when she visited schools, the first question the kids asked her was whether she was famous. So she wrote this poem about fame, playing with the question of what famous really meant, and the last lines of that poem became emblazoned on my mind—

"'I want to be famous in the way a pulley is famous, or a buttonhole, not because it did anything spectacular, but because it never forgot what it could do.'"

George remained silent for a second, then said, "Did you hear that? 'Famous because it never forgot what it could do.' You see, when we forget who and what really affects our lives—we are really forgetting what we can do. What we can do can only be done right here, right now, with each other. Over in that world of fame, where we *observe* life, experience it second-hand—from magazines, movies, TV shows, radio spots, pod casts—we can't know, and can't remember what we can do. We're not allowed to remember. That world over there is not real, no matter what the hype. It is carefully constructed to show only certain sides, a distorted image, of what is real. We can't make discoveries over there. We can't practice science over there. That *mediated* world teaches us how to stereotype, to pigeonhole. Those are the shortcuts to moving information fast, without allowing anyone to question it. In that mediated world people are categorized—by where they live, how much money they make—then sorted into groups and targeted with more *information.*

"Where all those categories end is the place where true creativity, true power and effectiveness, true *community*, begins. In a community, where you've chosen to be, you're free to do your most profound work. And that work is what builds nations, sends men to the moon, transforms waste, heals dreaded diseases, and grows great economies. That work, our work, is the expression of our inner story."

Putting his hand on his heart, George declared, "I promise you this, when we do our work, when we express our story, we create life. That is the stuff of actual raw hungry life. We create life because the telling of our story, in whatever way we have open to us, always builds relationships, and relationships are the very essence of life. Relationships are what make things happen. We're driven to express our story—to do our work—because we're driven to produce life. Life is here to create more life. I promise you this as a scientist. And I promise you this as a poet. We express our story to produce more stories. We express our life to produce more life.

"Find a teacher who loves to teach, or an entomologist who loves to observe bugs, or an actor who loves to act, or a chef who loves to cook, or anyone, anyone at all, who really loves what they do, and you'll find they don't spend a lot of time thinking about the meaning of life. That meaning is their life. It permeates their actions and is expressed in their story. It's only when we're removed from our work, or denied the opportunity to do it, that we cry for meaning.

"Often my father would ask my mother why she didn't sew her own clothes when she was so good at it. She'd tell him that she loved gardening, and the community of friends she shared her love of food with, more. And besides, she could make enough money from the fruits and vegetables she sold to buy the few clothes she needed. That was her idea of staying true to her heart and soul. She was clear that working with her hands in the earth gave her so much joy that she ended up earning more to have what she needed and wanted by sticking with what she loved to do. It meant more to her to produce food from the earth than clothes from a machine."

George shook his head sadly.

Chapter 5

"When we lose our meaning, we grow sick, really sick. The other thing about our work is that it is our link to the world. It is through our work that we build our web of connections and relationships. Somehow, when you're doing your work and expressing your story, you know that nothing you do, nothing you say or think, is for yourself alone. It just can never be for you alone. But when we're prevented from telling our story, from doing our work, we forget why we're doing what we're doing and become invisible.

"If you can't tell your own story, if you can't see yourself as part of a community of people, you can be certain that nobody else can either. Without friends, without relationships, we are invisible. You know me by who Donna is, by who Dusty, and Elizabeth are, and by who I was in my role at Terra. Without those, who would I be?

"Only you can know what your story is and who it is you serve. And if you don't know your purpose, your story, you can't create life. When you can't create life, you can't be strong.

"These nations and governments of ours, our schools, research labs, universities, businesses, corporations, and armies, our literature and art, all these are not built out of duty, obligation, loyalty or drive to prove ourselves. They are dynamic, living stories, our stories, yours, mine, and everyone's. They are the stories from our hearts, minds, and souls! And those things that we have in common—families, churches, clubs, and communities—are stories that we are telling together.

"And when we pretend that those stories are not about us, but about something outside of us, then we deny ourselves. When we try to let what we own substitute for telling our story, instead of ourselves, we die a little every day. We begin to forget who we are, our core purpose."

There was total silence at this gathering of friends and colleagues.

"And how did so many of us let go of our own stories? How did so many of us turn over the narrative of our life to someone else? When was it that we decided that we could no longer know for ourselves, and that others had to do the knowing for us? When was it that so many of us withdrew from our own experience and surrendered that right? Why have so many of us lost our sense of ourselves and come to let others define who we are and how we know?"

George raised his head and smiled.

"These questions would sound like mad ramblings in some circles. But that's because they've forgotten their stories and themselves. This loss of our sense of our self, of our confidence in our own ability to create and make things happen," George declared, pounding the podium for emphasis, "surrounds us and permeates our society!"

A strip of molding next to George's right hand popped off the top of the podium, fell to the stage, and bounced with a clatter. But no one noticed.

"But in order to change anything, we need a new language, a language for telling community stories full of symbol and meaning, community myths. A language that can take us where we never thought we could go. These myth stories won't come out of the electronic media that occupy so much of our time and attention. They must come from our own hearts and minds, with each of us doing our part, making our contribution.

"Tonight I'm not only ending my work as a research scientist at Terra, but starting a new chapter in my story, as Director of Business Graduate classes for Returning Students at Chelsea University.

"I will continue to use what I have learned, over so many years, to make a difference, to share what I know with the next generation.

"Right now, we speak a language of hardness—of hard realities, hard facts, hard divides, hard numbers, hard outcomes, hard work, and hard choices—right choice, wrong choice, cool or not cool."

George lifted a hand to his chin and stroked it gently.

"Think about that. How much hope for change is there in a world driven by cold, hard facts and figures? How much of us and our restless humanity can exist in a world defined by the language of these facts and figures... which is what most people think science is about. In reality, it is the judgment applied to the facts and figures along with our knowledge, wisdom and experience that allows scientists to make value decisions for companies like Terra."

George stepped around the lectern and edged up to the very end of the platform.

"I can tell you, as a scientist, that there is nothing about us that comes anywhere near to the hardness and finality we make over facts and figures. In fact, there is nothing about this world we inhabit that comes anywhere close to the illusions created by our language, the way it describes what we see and experience. We're not hard, and we have no finalities about us."

George threw a hand out, punctuating his words.

"The truth is that we have survived as a species because of our ability to make value judgments about the facts and figures before us, like my mother, who got more value from her gardening than her sewing. A life worth living is one where we are very clear about what we want, and are willing to pay the price to have it. Sometimes that price is material, and often it is not.

"But, it's our incredible capacity to change, to transform ourselves, from what we've believed we were to what we aspire to be, that is the foundation of our journey. It is our values that enable us to recreate ourselves as we make our way and maintain our aliveness.

"So, again, I have to ask myself as a scientist, and perhaps mostly as a scientist, why we have become so fixated on a language that runs counter to everything that we observe around us, a language that does not serve who we are and have always been. I am amused, for example, that all the life energy in our organizations and our corporations is still, to this day, characterized and often marginalized as the touchy-feely or soft issues. When we ignore or disempower the softness of real life, in favor of hard facts, metrics and statistics, we choose an elusive and often illusory certainty over real survival. To me, it's like constructing a skeletal system and expecting the rest of the body to magically appear and perform as it should."

George clasped his hands together and smiled impishly.

"Bottom lines, by themselves, do not a vision make! Profits don't happen because someone screams at workers to do the impossible."

George shook his head sadly.

"Those last years before Leonard were dark times at Terra, as many of you remember! Terra almost died, and who knows what would have happened to Chantilly if she had. A whole community almost lost its dreams and its future. But we didn't, and do you know why? Because our soft, flabby, irrepressible passion and values outlived the hardness of numbers. Our inner drive to move, to create, to play, to learn, and to adapt, transformed a dying company with a combined spirit that was stronger than the numbers that said there was nothing left!"

George turned and pointed dramatically at Leonard.

"In walked a leader who understood systems. Every

single day he would walk around the grounds and the plant buildings, having thoughtful conversations with every person. He treated all those relationships as if each one were as critical as veins flowing blood to the heart and arteries leading it away again. It was because of our relationships, because of the ones we built, that we were strong. Terra Waste Management, he explained over and over again, was a set of invisible, interdependent relationships. In other words, we all needed each other. Many people talk about partnerships, or collaborations leading to success, but Leonard Allegren taught us about integration, the way real sustainable systems work, and we sprang back to life. Leonard *was* the leader he wanted Terra to become.

George faced Leonard and began clapping. The entire hall stood and gave Leonard an ovation. Taken completely by surprise, Leonard flushed red.

"Now stop that blushing, Leonard!" George yelled. "It's my party and I'll humiliate whoever I want to."

After a lengthy applause, George raised the palm of one hand, and pressed the index finger of his other hand to his lips for silence.

McKenzie was staring at Leonard, startled by the crowd's enthusiastic show of gratitude. She had grown comfortable with her distaste for Leonard, and this outpouring of respect and affection conflicted with her preconceptions of who he was. It was unsettling and unwelcome, for it cracked that image in a way that she was not expecting. Then, George continued, and McKenzie turned her attention back to him.

"Leonard, I have one last thing to say about you this evening, and then I'm going to finish my speech. Even with all your grand strategic thinking and your constant push for improvement, you freed us! You freed us to tell our stories, and they have turned out to be far greater stories than we had ever imagined! You gave us the infrastructure, the foundations... the systems... to be all that we can be. And for that, we can all thank you.

Again, the hall burst into uproarious applause. George had used this moment, when all attention was focused on him and his retirement, to say what it was unspeakable to say in the everyday world of business. Its truth resonated with everyone gathered there that night. The applause for George, and the emotions behind them, were genuine and powerful.

"Remember Marshall McLuhan and his famous insight, 'The medium is the message?'" George asked, his eyes full of fire and challenge.

"Let me tell you a big secret, a secret so big that we've almost forgotten it. *The medium of life is commerce.* Commerce is the vehicle of life, ever-more-abundant life, full of ever-greater opportunities.

"Commerce has been the medium of life since the first basic elements exchanged goods and services with other basic elements to create a primitive system, and primitive systems exchange goods and services with other systems to create yet more powerful systems. This goes on and on, until this process exhibits what we recognize as life. Exchange is the method by which cells live and die. Life emerged from commerce, and what emerged from that commerce is soul, soul that embodied civilization, soul that created solutions to our most practical and basic physical needs, that drove our desires, and stirred the best and the worst in human beings. It is the soul that drives our spiritual yearning to understand more, to know more, to be more."

George straightened his entire body until the strength of his presence on this earth was palpable. He took a step back.

"This is where our forgetfulness has put us in jeop-

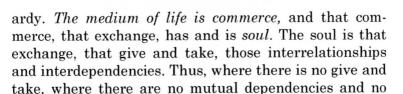
ardy. *The medium of life is commerce,* and that commerce, that exchange, has and is *soul.* The soul is that exchange, that give and take, those interrelationships and interdependencies. Thus, where there is no give and take, where there are no mutual dependencies and no reciprocity, there can be no soul."

George turned toward Leonard again.

"Leonard, for years now we have all heard you harp about the importance of building robust systems. And now, after all this time, I'm going to be presumptuous and tell you what you really meant by that obsession, what you didn't know yourself.

"Before you, Terra Waste Management existed *in* the world of commerce, but it was dying because there was no commerce *within* Terra. Your robust systems gave us commerce within our own environment, within our own life. They gave us our medium for give and take, for building our interrelationships and mutual dependencies. And this commerce forced its change on us. It delivered its message. It brought us life. It brought us back to our soul."

George turned back toward the audience, and at that moment, McKenzie understood that George was speaking as the entire community.

"This is what makes things happen—the web of relationships, of dependencies, of commerce. This is what pushes our ideas, our values, and our dreams into the world. This is the secret power that creates life—the web of commerce!"

Leonard was so intrigued by what George was saying that he forgot to camouflage his expression. If anyone had been watching him, they would have seen a Leonard no one had seen before.

"This life giving power of commerce is the force behind the real world, behind everything that happens. The same set of dynamics creates everything real that we can observe, whether it's an electron, a World War, or a vaccine. It's the same basic phenomenon—simple at its core, but stunning in its consequence."

Completely one with his message, George beamed out at the audience with a total absence of self-consciousness.

"This fabric of relationships, the warp and woof of our life, is behind the creation of everything we have ever experienced or ever will experience. The weaving of those relationships is the story of our life, and that restless process has a life of its own. We can feel it and experience it, but its dynamic complexity defies measurement and analysis. We can even zoom in and explore the tiniest portion of it. But we can never own it or control it, because we are part and parcel of it. We, ourselves, are the stuff of relationships.

It's not 'I think, therefore I am.' It's '*I relate, therefore I am.*' I exist because I am a web of relationships within a web of relationships. There is no 'I' but for those relationships, for without those relationships, there could be no activity, no commerce, no thing at all."

George gently adjusted his glasses and smiled.

"There is nothing that exists outside of a relationship, and the more it tries to, the more unreal it becomes. We live in a world—a universe—that emerges from relationships.

"Thus, when our relationships change, we change. When our relationships expand and grow stronger, we expand and grow stronger. When our relationships wither and die, we wither and die. You know the old saying about being careful about what you wish for because you might just get it. Well, let me tell you something. Be careful about what you choose to relate with because you most certainly will become it."

McKenzie's heart fluttered. She felt overwhelmed,

and a powerful image of a map of her relationships burst into her mind. McKenzie saw her connections with George, within that image, and wondered how George's words were affecting Leonard.

Curious, McKenzie gazed at Leonard, and found him studying George in open-mouthed wonder. And she wondered if, perhaps, Leonard was not quite the arrogant grandstander she had always thought. Then, George's voice jerked her out of her reverie.

"We know that we are alive because our relationships are always changing, into something new, something unexpected, always forcing us to reorganize ourselves and our lives. What goes around does, indeed, come around, but by the time it reaches our doorstep, it's different than it was over there when it was changing someone else."

With a big, knowing smile, George gently shook a finger at his audience and said, "You see, there is no such thing as a safe distance. No matter how remote they may seem to us, events, trends, movements, and actions of all kinds are already connected to us through a massive network of relationships—relationships so vast and encompassing that we don't see them. However, if we are to thrive, or even survive, in this maze of relationships, we must allow ourselves to know more than we ever thought we could know. We must develop our minds and our way of seeing and understandings things."

George stood very erect, a powerful presence dominating the room.

"We must learn to *love and respect life* in ways we never thought possible. We must be receptive to the *energy and vibrancy of life* as we never have been before. We must come to see ourselves as who and what we are—the purveyors, the very *agents of life*, rather than its observers and manipulators!"

George seemed to shrink on the stage as his inspiration withdrew.

"We must be *the soul of commerce!*"

Chapter 6

Communicating and Interacting With Others to Build a Common Language

"Strong communities...support the work of schools by providing educational and after-school activities for students. And strong communities nurture healthy children by surrounding them with a network of loving people who keep them safe and can guide them toward success. Forming what we call 'community coalitions' is an important step in reaching children who need help. Community coalitions bring together everyone from teachers, to mentors, to parents, to pastors, to police officers, to substance abuse experts, to social service providers, to business leaders. Anyone who has the ability and the desire to have a positive impact on a child's life should be part of a community coalition."

First Lady Laura Bush, at Avon Avenue School in Newark, March 16, 2006

Chapter 6

The boisterous applause that followed George's speech only heightened Leonard's inner turmoil. As he escorted George from the stage, he wondered what to do now. He'd known this day was coming and had tried to prepare for it. Amanda had started placing ads months ago, and when that didn't work, they gave the assignment to a recruiter, one of the best. Unfortunately, there just wasn't another George out there, and Leonard didn't know what they were going to do without him. The only choice might be to divide George's position into three separate jobs.

Leonard wouldn't have been quite so anxious if George had been the only key retiree he was having trouble replacing, but he wasn't.

Ten years before, when Leonard took over Terra Waste Management, everything seemed possible. Founded fifty years earlier, Terra had grown from a small, local, operation into a large business that transformed municipal, industrial, and agricultural waste into valuable products. Its main challenges when Leonard arrived were poor management and over specialization. Leonard solved the former with systems management, and George solved the latter by leading the R&D effort to develop new products from additional waste resources. That had led to a wave of controlled expansion, including the new divisions, *Terra Waste Consulting*, and *Green Communications*. There'd been ten years of growth, rising productivity, and increased profits. They'd all been so proud.

And all that time, the workforce problem had been lying there waiting.

As he handed George off to the crowd for some well-earned backslapping and hand shaking, Leonard wondered if he'd made the right decision in accepting the position as CEO of Terra. It had meant moving from a large city to a small one, but he had been drawn to the beauty of the surrounding mountains, and the challenge of a struggling business with excellent growth potential, a product he could be proud of, and the opportunity to do work that would make a real difference.

Leonard had always loved the outdoors life—he'd met his wife Alice at a ski lodge—and enjoyed the idea of making his livelihood by purifying and finding uses for wastes that would otherwise poison the landscape. Alice, of course, had been reluctant to leave the excitement of a big city for what she thought would be "the dull circles and odd characters" of a smaller city. But it was a good place, they thought, for their son to complete his education, and Alice's roses had thrived in the local soil.

Leonard and Alice joined the 'right' clubs and charities, made friends, and were accepted into the community. Everything seemed to be going well, at work and at home, until Bruce's behavior problems grew worse and McKenzie Jordan shifted the attention of her aggressive feature stories from the Terra's former leader to Leonard.

Donna finally managed to slip through the crowd to George, and Leonard turned and headed for Alice.

From Leonard's perspective, McKenzie's articles were pure mud slinging, mixing twisted fact with innuendo, sensationalizing the workforce problem, pointing to actions that, taken out of context, undermined him with his employees and with his board. If she didn't stop, Leonard stood to lose everything he'd worked for, and he knew, he knew, that he'd done everything he was supposed to do.

He served on the board of Chelsea University, allocated thousands of dollars every year for scholarships, opened internships up to countless people in the community, brought teachers in, and sponsored field trips. He even helped put together a workforce committee with the Greater Chelsea Chamber of Commerce, as many of the other members voiced the same recruitment problems. It wasn't just Terra. Just this year, the committee had done a survey of their membership's contributions to programs, projects, and scholarships, totaling over ten million dollars in the last five years. But none of it had made a measurable bit of difference. All any of the business leaders were sure about was that there were definitely more requests for more money.

Leonard had reached the edge of the crowd, only a few yards from Alice, when he was intercepted by McKenzie.

When McKenzie saw Leonard stepping down from the stage, she knew she had only a few moments to reach her elusive prey. Determined to get an appointment for a real interview, she turned from the stage and began weaving through the crowd toward Leonard's table.

Unfortunately, a retirement celebration—no matter how beloved the retiree—was not front-page material, especially not when there had been so many lately. But to McKenzie, the number of retirements wasn't the point. It was the fact that Terra was taking so long to replace them. Is this extensive lag time between new hires a signal that Terra is changing its local hiring commitments? To her, it was all a symptom of the rot in the business community, a rot centered on Terra Waste and Leonard Allegren. As she neared her goal, previous frustrated efforts to secure an interview crossed her mind. Leonard had treated the community like a busi-

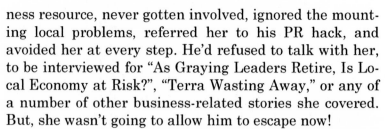

ness resource, never gotten involved, ignored the mounting local problems, referred her to his PR hack, and avoided her at every step. He'd refused to talk with her, to be interviewed for "As Graying Leaders Retire, Is Local Economy at Risk?", "Terra Wasting Away," or any of a number of other business-related stories she covered. But, she wasn't going to allow him to escape now!

McKenzie reached Leonard's table just as Leonard stepped out of the crowd.

Leonard stopped when McKenzie planted herself in front of him. He turned his gaze from his wife to McKenzie and asked, "Ms. Jordan?"

"It's time we talked personally, Mr. Allegren. I have my book; which day next week would work for you?"

"I don't *have* to—"

"My next article will be on 'A Wake for Terra Waste', and I think some input from its CEO would be of interest."

Letting out a long breath, Leonard said, "Very alliterative. Isn't George your friend too?"

"That's the society column. Mine won't even mention George, just what you're doing to Chantilly."

"I'm running a business, Ms. Jordan, a very fine one, that employs three times as many people as any other in town."

"And treats the people and the community like faceless 'resources'."

"I'm on the board of the University—"

"Ensuring they train students for jobs at Terra."

"Our scholarship program is—"

"---a way to bribe students to work for you."

"We give thousands to local—"

"Fundraiser photo ops."

"I'm a member of the Chamber—"

Chapter 6

"'Old boys' helping each other—"

"Our internships—"

"Cheap labor and training."

"The field trips—"

"Community relations."

"Alice is Past-President of the Garden—"

"Another photo op."

Leonard gasped, glared, drew himself up and declared, "Now that...I don't know why you dislike *me* McKenzie, but that's really crossing the line and you know it!" Leonard gestured past McKenzie's shoulder, toward his table and his wife and said, "Alice loves her roses, was very, very proud when the *Scarlet Leonard* took the blue ribbon," McKenzie flushed as Leonard continued, "and you didn't criticize the field trips when *you* were leading them."

"When I was naïve enough to believe you wanted to help the children."

"I did, I do, I'm doing everything I—"

"Then why don't you leave your glass tower and get involved with what is going on around you? All my research says that finding and keeping good people is becoming incredibly difficult, and you can't grow your own. You're going to have to become involved with the community, where the people come from. Let's make our first interview about this."

As he glared down at her, Leonard realized, for the first time, that McKenzie was honestly worried about Chantilly, and thought *he* was part of the problem. He recalled part of George's speech and asked, "Is *that* what you believe, McKenzie? I thought..."

"That I was trying to advance my career? Move up to a bigger station or newspaper? *This* is my *home*, Leonard."

Frowning in puzzlement, Leonard said, "Maybe... I may have misunderstood you, McKenzie. Will you accept that you may have misunderstood me?"

At that moment they finally noticed that the party sounds had faded, and they looked up to find that nearly everyone was staring at them, grinning in open amusement. They were saved from further embarrassment by George, who stepped out of the crowd with Donna on his arm and yelled, "Is anyone else hungry? Let's eat!" He nodded to McKenzie, said, "Later, McKenzie," and led Leonard back to Alice.

Chapter 7

Integrated Systems Thinking

"B.F. Skinner emphasized a first principle of scientific methodologists: when you find something interesting, drop everything else and study it. Too many fail to answer opportunity's knock at the door because they have to finish some preconceived plan. Creative geniuses do not wait for the gifts of chance; instead, they actively seek the accidental discovery."

Michael Michalko, *A Theory About Genius*

Chapter 7

The glow of George's retirement party lingered in Chantilly for quite some time. Even two weeks later, it was still possible to overhear locals trading remarks, at the corner coffee shop, about the grandeur of the event, who was there, and most of all, what George had said. Topics of particular interest among the wagging tongues included George's increased presence in the community life, and his honoring of Leonard.

On this particular morning, as Leonard pulled into a 'visitor' spot at Chelsea University, he was looking forward to seeing his friend and close confidante again, and to getting a better understanding of what George hoped to accomplish with his new students. George had always been ahead of everyone at Terra with his ideas on how to keep things moving, and Leonard hoped to learn how to help out his friend.

George and Donna had just returned from a vacation/second honeymoon in George's native Costa Rica. They had purchased a "retirement" home there, and George had begun making plans and developing contacts for a cooperative Student Exchange program with a branch of the Universidad de Costa Rica. But this first trip was for pure pleasure.

Leonard strode up the steps to the top of the Chelsea University Research and Development building. He and George had agreed to meet in the corridor a little early, to exchange information about what George wanted from him on his first visit with George's graduate class in Systems Thinking for Business Management. It was Leonard's first visit to the new building, but George's directions were clear and accurate.

George, typically early, was waiting patiently, and grinned when he saw Leonard's head appear in the stair well.

"Good morning Leonard," George said, "welcome to ST560. All 5 of my students are eagerly waiting to share their work with you, our expert on systems integration."

"Morning George. How was the trip?"

"Excellent! We had a great time, my family was proud, and we were the talk of my old neighborhood—a poor boy who left home for the opportunities of *el norte* returns years later with money and a beautiful wife."

"Great! How are your students?"

"They'll probably have a lot of questions, but please do me a favor and be sure to ask them questions as well. A key objective of the course is ensuring that the students develop their own set of creative, critical thinking skills. You pushing them to 'think for themselves', will help them a lot. Frankly, I think you'll find this to be a bright bunch when it comes to understanding the technology.

That said, they don't quite understand yet what it takes to put everything together as a system to solve any problems. But they're getting there. This should be fun....are you ready?"

"Yep."

As they entered the classroom, Leonard saw the five students—three men and two women—seated around a large flat panel LCD monitor, focusing on a 3D multicolored map, which Leonard thought he recognized. It looked like a bit like a system of mountain ranges that converged at many intersections.

George said, "Ladies and gentlemen, I'd like you to meet one of the foremost experts on applying a systems model in the business community, Mr. Leonard Allegren."

They turned, smiled and one by one shook Leonard's hand and exchanged a brief greeting.

"So what are you looking at?" asked Leonard with interest.

Chapter 7

Tom, seated at the keyboard, said, "This is a three dimensional map that shows the volume of liquid sewage produced by grid in each part of Chantilly. We're using the latest GIS software."

"Professor Aguilera got it for us, said Somer, a rosy-cheeked brunette.

Tom said, "We're just learning how to download data and see if we can understand what it's telling us about the sewage system Terra operates."

Leonard, grinned and said, "Well this should be interesting. Let's talk about it for a minute."

He looked around at their faces, letting thoughts percolate about where to begin and then said, "First, let's talk about the system you're studying and how you would define what it is. Then, we'll go a little further and discuss the specific characteristics of the elements of a system. What are the boundaries of a system? Who do you think the stakeholders are? How would you define them and what are the key relationships between the stakeholders? Last, we'll talk about some of the exchanges that are important for a system to be successful."

George, smiled broadly and he listened and watched Leonard the business leader, transformed into a master teacher, crafted his questions as if he was helping his employees learn a new concept or thought process.

Somer hesitated slightly, but was the first to respond, as she replied, "Like Tom said, we're studying the sewage system of Chantilly. It has the physical properties of pipes that connect all of the elements, a set of rules by which the sewage flows from one part to another, a set of chemical processes that modify the form of sewage as it moves through the system, and a set of boundaries that it operates within."

"What's the purpose of the system?" quizzed Leonard.

"To transform Chantilly generated sewage into water that can be returned to the water system and by-products that can be sold in the market." replied Somer.

Leonard paused, to mull over Somer's response and said, "Somer, that's a darn good definition. You included the boundaries of the system, the goal or purpose of the system, the relationship to another system, and hinted at an exchange.

Leonard turned to the others and asked, "Are there stakeholders in the system?"

Harry replied, "Well, the stakeholders, those who will be affected by what happens with this sewage system, include Terra—because the company has a contract with the city to purify water for a fee—and of course Chantilly, because it's buying the service and getting clean water."

Leonard nodded and said, "That's a good start. We'll come back to that question again a little later.

"Now, how can you use the GIS system to improve this system's performance?"

Somer raised a hand and replied, "We know that improving the system not only requires that everyone understands how it operates, but also that when you make a change, you have to understand the total system impact—depending on your boundaries of course. Changing one thing could have some unintended consequences on other parts of the system. The GIS helps us create a model of the system stakeholders, their interactions or interface, gather data about system performance, it helps us understand the system boundaries, and it allows us to get a sense of what changes might do within the boundaries we have set. It's a great modeling and analysis tool that we can then apply judgment to."

Leonard smiled and thought about what a wonderful job George was doing...he had easily moved from the

Chapter 7

teacher scientist at Terra to the teacher scientist at Chelsea U. He wondered how many of these students knew that they were stakeholders also.

The exchange of questions and answers on and key thoughts about systems continued for the next forty minutes.

Chapter 8

Becoming a Stakeholder

Your Presence is Often More Valuable than your Pocketbook.

Chapter 8

Trevor pounded his gavel, bellowed a welcome, and called the meeting to order. The Lyceum members and visitor quickly settled. Trevor led them in their Pledge and opened the meeting. Then he stood, turned to his right and said, "Come on George."

George stood, facing Trevor and Trevor said, "As the outgoing Chair, I hereby turn our gavel over to you. May it continue to serve Chantilly in your hands." The members stood and clapped enthusiastically, including the visitor, Leonard.

Leonard had never seen any value or relationship with his business and the weekly Lyceum meetings, so he hadn't bothered to attend them. But now that his good friend George was retired and had finally allowed them to elect him Chair, Leonard couldn't refuse the invitation to the installation. So, there he was, seated in the back with other business types, next to the President of the Chamber, Ted Bruer, watching a mix of community leaders congratulate George.

Leonard had a foggy notion that the Lyceum was a sort of roundtable discussion group focused on community affairs. He'd been surprised to see McKenzie seated at the front table, to the left of George, taking notes. But his suspicious speculations were interrupted by George's acceptance speech.

George stood behind the sturdy lectern, clasped its edges in both hands, leaned toward the audience and said, "I came to Chantilly forty-five years ago. I'd been looking for work that would enable me to complete my education, and found a manual labor job with a small, new, 'garbage recycling' company. I worked hard, took night classes, and completed my degree. With the ink still damp on my sheepskin, I began looking for an engineering job, just as, with the help of Chantilly Capital..." George nodded to Trevor and continued, "...my original employer merged with a competitor and renamed itself 'Terra Waste Management'. I applied for and won a position in product development, continued my studies, earned my Masters and Doctorate, and met and married Donna. We started a family, and as we raised our kids, I worked my way up the ladder of the growing company, eventually becoming the Head of R&D. I received a lot of help along the way, and now that I'm retired, I can finally devote my full time to serving this community that has meant so much to me and my family. Trevor, fellow members, you've been asking me to accept this Chair for ten years, and now, finally, I am very pleased to accept."

Puzzled, Leonard leaned over and whispered to Ted, "Just how does the Lyceum serve the community?"

Ted gazed off to the side in thought for a few moments, and then whispered back, "Well, first you have to understand what the Lyceum is. A lot of people assume it's another service club, one of those that picks a project, a disease or something, and raises money for it. But our members come from the entire community and work to serve the entire community, on projects they choose, because they believe it's important to the whole community.

"Specifically, what we do is look at the community as a whole system, as representative stakeholders who have an interest in that system—either because we will be affected by whatever strategy we agree to, because we have resources invested in some way, or because we have special knowledge that will influence the outcome. There are no absolute rules or boundaries about the limits of the 'system'—the projects chosen or the members who participate. The aim however is clear—it should be inclusive and broad rather than the opposite."

Chapter 8

Leonard took a moment to digest that and said, "Wow, you sure fired that off quick."

Ted grinned and replied, "Well, I've been a member for, oh, thirty years now."

Leonard asked, "So what does that mean in practical terms?"

"Well, we examine community problems, especially like those we've posted to that board to our left," he said, pointing to a large white board on the wall near the podium.

"We think of some of them ourselves, and some are brought to us by community members. We have retreats, training programs, lectures—our upcoming speaker, Dr. Stephen Glenn is all about helping the community learn how to help kids do better. He has more than twenty years of research on why our kids aren't doing so well today. And if we take on a community-wide project, we take a 'whole system approach' approach to it."

Leonard nodded and said, "Oh, well, I understand that. George would be a natural leader for this."

"He was one of the founders."

Leonard chuckled quietly and said, "Somehow I'm not surprised. How do you choose members?"

"We don't, people select themselves."

Trevor stood again, shook George's hand, and the members stood and applauded again. During the applause, Leonard leaned over and whispered to Ted, "They look like old friends."

As George began the routine announcements, Ted whispered, "You don't know? Of course, you weren't here then. That would have been just after the first Gulf War; Trevor was in that one as a First Lieutenant. After he was discharged he became a Senior Account Manager at Chantilly Capital...had the Terra account when they applied for another loan. They wanted to expand their way out of their problems."

George was leading a discussion of ambassador candidates, focusing on who would be appropriate for various issues such as 'overseas education'.

Leonard whispered, "Just before the Board recruited me?"

"Yes. Under George the small R&D team had developed leading-edge treatment and reclamation processes for agricultural waste, but Terra's old management didn't know how to implement the processes or develop the market. When they went to Chantilly Capital for more funding, Trevor investigated Terra and met George. George explained everything from the engineering side. Trevor investigated the potential market, and agreed to the loan on condition that Terra's Board brought in a CEO who was up to the job."

"So that was why…"

"That was the excuse the Board needed. The guy before you, Dan, was a decent mechanical engineer, but he didn't understand sales or systems, and Terra got too big for him to handle.

"They needed someone who understood business, a systems management type.

"I wouldn't know about that. But, you know George. He and Trevor got on well and became close friends. Trevor went on to make a bundle at Chantilly Capital, and a lot of local contacts. He left there to begin a career in local politics, and that's how he wound up as Mayor."

Mrs. S.J. Dakota launched into one of her rants on the state of our academic institutions, supported by her daughters, Darla and Christy. Having heard it all before, most members gave her only polite attention, with the usual exception of Dr. Maureen McMahon, President of Chelsea University.

Giving the spirited discussion only part of his atten-

Chapter 8

tion, Leonard asked, "What's Ms. Jordan doing up there?"

"McKenzie? Well...let's see... right. She became involved in community activities when she was the Journalism teacher at Wheaton High. Encouraged the kids to get involved in the community—investigate things, find out what was going on and how things worked. I used to have teenagers coming into my feedlot looking for a story—until she was pushed out again."

"Pushed? Again?"

"You see, she got her start as an aide at Chantilly Grade School, while completing her degree. English, I think. Wanted to be in charge of a class, to 'make a difference.' So then she completed her degree and got a class. Was a real innovative teacher too. Got some special training in how the brain works or develops or something, and she's been working on that angle for a long time, partly because of Isabel. Have you seen Isabel's picture yet?"

"Isabel? Who's that?"

"Oh, thought you knew. Well, she's the little girl from Costa Rica, well, not so little now, that McKenzie has supported for—"

"Costa Rica? That's where George was from originally. They just bought a retirement home there."

"Yeah, that's right. Anyway, it's a long story. McKenzie left elementary teaching when the state increased the focus on core subjects like reading and math, started teaching to tests, eliminated the field trips, put the squeeze on recess, and well... You should hear her talk about it sometime. She thinks all that is crazy, because, let's see, she says something like 80% of all nerve endings in the hands tie directly to the brain, and kids need to be learning with their hands and feet, and 'not their b...s'. Well... anyway, she can get real heated about 'hands-on learning, and when they cut that, she left."

Leonard said, "So that was the first time. What happened after that? She was 'pushed' again?"

"Oh... there was a hunting accident, and they needed a journalism teacher at Wheaton High. McKenzie was the only teacher who could take the job mid-year, so they gave her an emergency certification."

"After they published that article on Terra in the Wheaton High paper, her contract wasn't renewed and she had to find another job."

"What article?"

"You didn't hear about that either? You *have* to get out more. It was one of the things that brought you here, and it won a bunch of awards, from state and national education and news groups.

"Let's see... a, couple of her student reporters decided to investigate Terra and see what was 'really' behind their financial problems. The students were an idealistic bunch, tenacious as terriers, and, of course, their parents had a lot to lose if Terra went under."

"They worked there?"

"A lot of the parents did, and most of the rest owned Terra stock. We like to keep our money local, including our retirement savings."

Leonard said, "Terra's stock dropped over 40% before they hired me."

"Everyone was afraid it was going under. The local economy depended on Terra, and a lot of us were invested in it. It was McKenzie and her kids, though, who broke the story about the deal with Chantilly Capital. Embarrassed the Chronicle, but gave hope to everyone else."

Leonard said, "There was a lot of glad handing when Alice and I arrived."

"We were depending on you."

Chapter 8

Houston Campbell stood and George recognized him. An older man with rugged features and a working pair of cowboy boots, he was a respected high-tech cattle rancher, he calmly suggested that S.J. and Dr. McMahon settle down and listen to each other.

When Houston finished, Leonard whispered, "Sounds like McKenzie enjoyed teaching. Why'd she leave?"

"Her heart went out of it when they cut the field trips, part of the statewide focus on 'basic'. That would have been, oh, a year or two after you started at Terra."

"I remember having her class out once."

Ted said, "I miss having the kids out to my place. They used to take them out to farms, my feedlot, the mill—let 'em milk a cow, shuck corn, that sort of thing. But they stopped that, and now the kids don't understand where things come from."

"I don't recall hearing about McKenzie for a couple years."

"She took a couple years off to write her book."

"Book?"

"Losing Heart in Education."

"Interesting...how'd she earn a living?"

"Part time fact checker for the Chronicle. They wanted her full time, as a reporter, but she insisted on finishing the book first."

"How'd it do?"

"The book? Everybody around here loved it."

"So what did she say was wrong with education?"

Ted grinned and replied, "According to her it's not just education, but she explains it better than I could. Read the book; they have a couple copies in the library, or ask her."

Leonard considered his current hiring problems, the fact that he wasn't finding solutions in the business environment and said, "You know, I just might."

Leonard turned his full attention to the discussion. Houston had the floor again and was saying, "...need people who don't have to be told every blasted step to take to get a job done. The cowboys are gone and with them went men who could apply what they knew in practical ways. Today we have people who have degrees in range animal husbandry, animal science, agricultural science, horticulture, plant and soil science and they can't do squat. I know we need engineers, scientists, and managers, but they've got to be able to apply what they learn right where the problem is. Otherwise it's of no value and we're not getting them. Twenty-six percent of the students who start eighth grade drop out before graduating high school—too many damn video games— and those that finish college aren't worth a damn either. They don't know anything useful, they can't do anything, they can't think, they aren't responsible, and they don't know how to work!"

The Lyceum went silent, and Leonard sat up straight in amazement. The local cattle ranchers were having the same workforce problems as Terra.

A middle-age woman in a pantsuit shot to her feet, demanding recognition. Leonard leaned toward Ted, who whispered, "Dr. Edra Brode, the School Superintendent."

George recognized her and she said, "Despite Houston's figures, the high school drop out rate is only 2% of the current graduating class."

Houston retorted, "What happened to the other 24% Edra? The ones who turned 18 and didn't bother to show up at school anymore? Don't they count? Or do you just call it 'shrinkage', like they do in retail?"

While the audience laughed, Leonard leaned toward Ted and whispered, "What's going on?"

Ted whispered back, "Old argument; different perspectives and goals, different figures and interpretations. S.J., Houston, and Edra have been fighting about it for years."

Leonard replied, "At Terra, we'd stop arguing and examine the basics, look for root causes."

Ted said, "So tell them."

"I'm just a visitor."

"Go ahead. It's an open forum; anyone can speak."

Leonard took a moment to organize his thoughts, and stood up. Behind the podium, George grinned, signaled Edra to wind up her rebuttal and said, "Leonard?"

"Thank you for inviting me tonight, George. I've been listening to what everyone has said, and a couple things sand out for me. I was surprised to find that Houston and others, in businesses very different from mine, are having the same kind of workforce issues. It sounds like the problem is pervasive and growing.

"In addition, it sounds like no one has any idea how big this issue is, what's causing it, how to solve it, or even how to measure it. I empathize with all of you, because I don't either.

"Of course, some of us are facing the issue as parents, others as educators, and others as business people, each with our own perspectives and assumptions. We each have our view of the elephant.

"Now at Terra when we have a problem like this, say between management, engineering, manufacturing, and sales, we'd stop and ask ourselves some basic, fundamental, questions like 'What's the process?' 'What metrics are we measuring?' and 'Is the process in control?'

"As far as education is concerned, I'm beginning to wonder if I'm part of the problem. We keep getting requests for money to help 'fix' the schools, and, as Dr. McMahon and Dr. Brode know, we give generously every year. But no matter how much we give, it never seems to help. Kids still drop out, and those who finish don't have the skills we need and don't seem able to learn them. Why? Is it our children? The schools? The environment? The work? What is it? I don't know, but we *have* to find out. Arguing about the metrics won't solve the problem. We have to decide what the problem is and find a solution!

Still grinning, George asked, "Leonard, are you offering to join the Lyceum in its effort to solve this?"

"Well, I guess, yes."

"Fellow Lyceum members, I hereby propose Leonard Allegren, a respected member of this community known to all here, for membership in Lyceum number 127, located in the township of Chantilly. Do we have a second? Ted?"

"I second the motion."

"The motion is accepted. All in favor, so indicate by saying 'aye'."

"Aye!"

"Opposed?"

...

George's gavel struck the podium with a loud "crack," and George declared, "The ayes have it. Leonard, welcome to the Lyceum."

When the meeting ended, Leonard joined the others in congratulating George and received welcoming handshakes himself. The last to approach him was McKenzie, whose open, welcoming smile surprised and relieved him. When she finished her greeting, Leonard thanked her and said, "I was talking with Ted. Do you have a few minutes?"

"Sure. What's on your mind?"

"You've been interested in Terra since long before I arrived, haven't you?"

Chapter 8

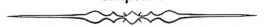

"Of course, 'as goes Terra, so goes Chantilly'. It's never been about you, Leonard, but the community."

"So, was I an improvement?"

"You injected new life into 'Terra-ble Waste of Money'."

"I never heard it called that."

"Of course not. Do you realize how little you talk with the people of Chantilly about what Terra means to us?"

"Most of the time when someone from the community talks with me, they want money for some 'good cause.' It's like all Terra is to this town is an ATM."

"And what else do you give to the community? What about your time, your self? The only time any of us see you is at high-society socials or business meetings, the sort of events where you don't see school teachers or grocery clerks. It's as though you're not really part of Chantilly, and because you don't know us, your business plans don't include us."

"Is that why you cover Terra from so many angles?"

"It's been the only way to reach you."

"Reach me? Not only did you reach me, but you reached everyone else. Do you realize what your headlines, editorials, and exposes have been doing to our stock? To my career?"

"Was I right?"

"That's not the point! The citizens of Chantilly are a major stockholder block. The Chronicle has a huge effect on local opinion, and every expose you print hurts us and makes my job harder!"

"It was the only way to get Terra to communicate with us."

"I have a lot of communications tools—phone, email, fax, cell, PDA, 'net access—that keep me up to the minute on real-time activity. It's improved my productivity so much that I can attend community functions like Lyceum."

McKenzie sighed and said, "I'm not talking about

electronic communications tools. You don't really touch people with those. I'm talking about the tools of personal communication, like face to face conversations, that build real relationships. Remember George's speech?"

Leonard replied, "The time for that is when I'm about to make an important business decision. I need to see the whites of their eyes and sense what's going on in their guts before closing. You have to do that in person."

McKenzie smiled and said, "Exactly. Look, we have very different ideas about what the word 'communication' means. It sounds like, for you, it's data flowing over electronic pathways. So in order to improve your 'communication', you outfit yourself, and Terra, with more and better technical data streaming tools. You have more communications equipment than a pit crew at the Indy 500®.

"I'm not saying there's anything wrong with that. I have a PDA myself. But for me, communications is about the exchange of thoughtful messages that shape peoples ideas and influence the way that they think.

"Obviously I use data, but the goal of my communication is to deliver a message that moves people to action."

Leonard smiled and said, "I use data to move people to action every day. In fact, I can reach anyone and everyone at Terra at any time."

McKenzie said, "And why do you have personal contact before signing a deal with someone? You already know what's missing from your communications tools. I'm just saying that in order to get to know Chantilly, to truly understand us, you have to communicate with us with the same degree of intimacy you would use in a business deal—real, personal, contact."

Taken aback, Leonard was caught in thought for a moment.

"Leonard," McKenzie continued, "one thing we have

in common is that we both care about this community, right?"

Leonard continued staring into space, but nodded and McKenzie said, "But while you've been busy moving electrons, you've missed a crucial part of the communication process, crafting the message you want people to hear."

Leonard frowned, nodded again and replied, "OK, so, you're a journalist, and I'm a businessman. Communication is something we both do every day and feel we're pretty good at. After all, your articles sell newspapers, and Terra is making money. But our sense of 'communication' is very different. For me it's about gathering facts and data, so that I can make business decisions and give directions. For you, it's about crafting the message. Same word, different meanings."

"Not bad for a businessman," quipped McKenzie.

"OK, so what's your message to me about Terra Waste Management?"

McKenzie grinned and said, "Not so fast. I'm not through with 'communication' yet. You techno wizards want to get to what you *think* is the heart of an issue and move on without really understanding the significance of what you just learned and what people think about it.

"Think for a moment about the number of times you've heard someone use a word that painted a picture in your mind about what they meant. Then later in the conversation, they headed off on a complete tangent. Sometimes that's because the conversation you think you are having with them is not the one they think they are having with you."

Leonard replied, "Like the point Houston was trying to make about Edra's report. Edra was using her definition of 'drop-out rate', and Houston was talking about the reality of kids not being in school."

McKenzie responded, "Right! That's a very good example of two people using exactly the same word, but with a different meaning, and thus not communicating."

Leonard's PDA began to vibrate, reminding him of the appointment with Dr. Gedissman and he said, "I have to go, but we really need to talk. Let's continue this on Monday, alright? Oh..." Leonard reached into his coat pocket, pulled out a business card, handed it to McKenzie and said, "Next time you have a question about Terra, please call me directly. I'll do my best to 'communicate', the way you mean it."

After they bade each other goodbye, Leonard pulled out his cell and called Amanda, the head or H.R. at Terra. "Amanda," he said, "I need an update of our latest hiring metrics. Get the team together and let's review it tomorrow morning. Confirm the time with Jane."

After dinner that evening, Leonard and Alice met in the kitchen while cleaning up. Leonard said, "I thought the meeting with Dr. Gedissman went well."

Alice dropped the pans in the sink with a loud clatter and her voice rose, as she said, "At least he gave us some options."

Pausing to consider her words, Leonard gently responded, "Well, I'm at least relieved. It didn't feel like he was selling us on *the drug* solution, like the school did."

With a sense of growing resignation that she would be shouldering most of the burden, Alice replied, "It gives us a lot more to do. Support groups and internet sites were only a beginning. Treatment programs, camps, classes for Bruce and us..."

Leonard blurted out, "Did you ever see so much stuff

Chapter 8

for sale? A.D.D.'s a *big* business." A thought he probably shouldn't have voiced.

But fortunately for future domestic tranquility, at that moment, Bruce screeched, "Mooommm!" from the back of the house.

Seeking the Soul of Commerce

Chapter 9

Conceptualize Information and Reorganize

"We trained hard...but it seemed that every time we were beginning to form up into teams we would be reorganized. I was to learn later in life that we tend to meet any new situation by reorganizing, and what a wonderful method it can be for creating the illusion of progress while producing confusion, inefficiency, and demoralization.

"Petronius Arbiter, Roman Legionnaire, 210 B.C."

Seeking the Soul of Commerce

Chapter 9

It was early morning as Leonard slid Millie into his Terra parking space and said into his cell, "... whole new side to George. With him in charge, this Lyceum group will listen."

...

"Because they had new perspectives, you know systems thinking, to social issues beyond research or product development. He thinks about the lives of real people."

...

"Show me I'm wrong. 'It's crazy to keep trying the same old thing when it keeps not working.' Look, I'll be there in two, and if you don't have anyone for us, we'll have to try *something* different!"

Leonard snapped his cell shut, removed his earphone, and slid both into his coat pocket.

Less than two minutes later, he strode into the executive conference room. Amanda Caldwell and the rest of the H.R. team were waiting for him around the table.

As he moved to a seat at the table, Leonard thanked everyone for coming in early and asked, "OK, Amanda, what do our current hiring metrics look like?"

Amanda stood, and walked to the foot of the table, holding a laser pointer. She faced Leonard and said, "Our workforce problem appears to be twofold—decreasing recruitment and increasing loss.

"Recruiting is becoming increasingly difficult because the capabilities of new workers have been dropping for decades. While there are plenty of people looking for work; they just don't seem to have the skills and abilities we need.

"Simultaneously, we're losing more and more of our experienced, technically savvy personnel—many to retirement, while some are being lured away—and it's becoming harder and harder to replace them. It often takes 3 new hires to do the work of one of the older, savvy workers. At first, as it became harder to find people, we simply expanded our recruitment efforts from local to regional, and regional to national, pools of candidates. But at this point, none of these efforts are working well."

"Why not?"

"Well, we'd assumed at first that it was a local problem, but when our national efforts came up short, we investigated and discovered a universal problem that's going to affect every business and industry."

Leonard said, "That's rather melodramatic."

"But accurate." Amanda nodded to one of her co-workers, who lifted a remote. The lights dimmed, and a PowerPoint image appeared on the large screen on the wall behind Amanda. She stepped to the side, pointed at the image with her laser and said, "This curve illustrates the average age of our employees. As you can see, the peak is at just over 53, but this is somewhat deceptive. When we eliminate non-technical employees and those with less than ten years experience, we get this."

A second image appeared. Amanda pointed again and said, "As you can see here, our critical peak for experienced, technically savvy employees is above 57."

Leonard stared and said, "Half of them will reach retirement age over the next eight years?"

"Yes, but that's not the worst of it. We'd be fine if we could replace those people. But if something doesn't change, we won't be able to—not enough of them."

"What! Why?"

"Supply and demand. The pool of experienced, technical personnel—national and regional—is shrinking rapidly, while the demand for them is growing. That's why we're having trouble replacing our retirees, and it's only going to get worse."

"What about younger kids? With five, eight, years of training and experience..."

Amanda shook her head, waved to her associate, and another image appeared. "The number of technically trained or trainable employees entering the workforce is also shrinking. The total number of school children also went down in the 1980s, from a high of 50 million in 1970 to a low of about 40 million. While the numbers have gone up some this last year, we still haven't figured out why the programs of the last 40 years haven't worked. So there's little point being optimistic about a rise in the population if we don't have a grip on how to prepare them."

Leonard said, "So there's a shortage of young, experienced workers now, but not in the future?"

"That's part right. Experience will still be an issue in the future, if we don't find a solution to the skills and abilities problem.

"Now, Chantilly is part of the national statistical pattern. The total number of students is back up now, but the crucial demographics have changed. For instance, back in the 1950s almost 12% of college degrees, across the U.S., were in engineering; now it's down to 5.5%. And of the remaining 5.5%, 43% are foreign born and usually here on temporary student visas...netting in the entire U.S. just over 3%. We're seeing the same decline across the board in technical education. Of the few who choose technical degrees, far too many are completely unprepared to solve real-world problems.

"In fact, the results of a survey of parents and their students that was published just days ago showed that 4 out of 10 young people would be very unhappy if they had to go into a career that was heavily dependent on math and science capabilities. At least half of those surveyed said they didn't think they needed, nor did they want, any more math and science instruction. Frankly, that attitude scares me, and it affects us.

"Look at these recent applicants."

The image and CV of a young man appeared on the screen and Leonard said, "Curtis Mathews. I interviewed him two weeks ago."

Amanda nodded and replied, "For one of the 'Industrial Site Dismantling' positions. He was the best of twenty-two 'possibles'. Why didn't you hire him?"

"He scored too low in 'creative thinking'."

Another image and CV appeared on the screen, of an equally young woman. Leonard said, "Celestina Gonzalez, WasteWater Treatment Engineer."

Amanda replied, "The most qualified of sixteen possible candidates."

Leonard nodded and said, "Her critical and creative thinking scores were ok, but her psych profile indicated immature socialization. She couldn't relate with other people, only machines."

A third image and CV appeared, of a handsome young man in a dark suit. Leonard said, "Jason Wrigley, for the Management Trainee position. Couldn't grasp 'systems thinking', and his social skills were little better than Celestina's."

Amanda nodded and said, "And those were the 'best' candidates. Most of the others scored so low in basic skills they couldn't be considered."

"Basic skills?"

"Reading comprehension, technical and creative writing, math, teamwork—the basic skills we need in all our salaried employees. They've been falling for decades."

Leonard frowned deeply and asked, "Is the solution to move business out of the country?"

Chapter 9

Amanda shook her head vigorously and said, "Not on your life. The problems we're having also exist in other countries; we're just seeing the biggest impact of them here in the U.S. first."

"Yikes!" said Leonard. He stroked his chin for a bit and said, "I don't understand this. We donate tens of thousands to Chelsea University each year, endowed a couple chairs, support the technical training we need. We've set up computer labs in all the schools, and yet the number and quality of graduates is going down?"

Amanda frowned and replied, "Yes. While the pool of technical employees entering the workforce has been shrinking, the critical and creative thinking abilities and social skills of those who do enter it has been declining as well."

Leonard shook his head and said, "Leaving us with a critical undersupply of future managers and innovators. What's causing this?"

"We don't know, but it's not just us."

"Is it their education?"

"We don't think so. From the day they start school to the day they graduate, only 12% of a students time is spent in receiving classroom instruction—assuming they're in school every day, and receiving instruction 100% of the time they're there. Of course, there are a lot of other influences in their lives, so we can't realistically blame their lack of thinking and social skills on just what they get in a classroom."

Leonard said, "So it's not just the knowledge."

Amanda replied, "That's right. There are a lot of what we would assume to be bright, well-educated kids out there, if you only count diplomas. And, if all they needed was training in our industry, we could do that, if we had to. But, our success demands more than that."

Leonard nodded, then stood up and paced around

the room, quickly scanning the faces around the table, as he internally processed all that he had heard.

Breaking the silence, he said, "So what we need, then, is a way to find, or...what? Produce creative, critical, thinkers who can relate and work effectively with other people? Maybe *we* can't do it, but somebody used to. All our best people came from somewhere. What changed? What has to be changed? How and by whom? How do we get this done?

"It looks like we have some great data, but the problem is finding a solution. It's not clear we know enough about the root cause...we may only be seeing just the symptoms of a deeper problem. Amanda, I think we need some help. Why don't you keep asking questions, locally and regionally, about who else is having the same issues, and see if anyone is making some progress in this area. I don't know if I'm relieved or dismayed, but you've convinced me this isn't just a Terra problem. It's a much, much bigger issue. I'll ask some questions too, and we'll get back together next week."

Leonard left the conference room and headed for his office. On the way, he took his cell out of his pocket and called Dr. Maureen McMahon, President of Chelsea University. She wasn't in, but rang back just as he was sitting behind his desk and said, "Howdy, how are you doing, Leonard?"

"Hello Maureen, just a follow up to that Lyceum meeting."

"That's right; it was your first time. Congratulations on joining, by the way. You'll make a good addition."

"Thanks, I'm looking forward to it. What did you think of Houston and S.J.'s argument?"

"About education? They've been polarized over that

for years. Never can agree, but it makes for lively discussions. Was there something in particular you found
interesting?"

"We're having our own workforce problems at Terra,
and I was wondering if the University might be able to
help us."

"OK. How?"

"Well, you know we're having trouble replacing some
of our key people. My H.R. Director, Amanda, and her
team have used all the usual recruitment strategies—
placed ads, offered employment bounties, starting bo-
nuses, moving expenses, retained recruiters, etc. We've
received thousands of applications as a result, but not
from the 'right' people. Now, I've learned recently that
there seem to be two basic reasons for this. First, there
are a lot fewer technical graduates than there used to
be, and second, few of the graduates with the right
technical background have the skill sets we need."

"I appreciate your problem Leonard, and, if it makes
you feel any better, I can confirm it's not just Terra. I've
been contacted by a number of businesses with similar
workforce problems, but you've been more specific. Not
just the numbers of applicants, but their skill sets…like
what?"

"Yes, it's a complex, multifaceted problem. What we
need are technically trained people who can apply their
knowledge to problems they've not seen before. If I were
to make a list, they would have at least the following
eight skills—

"The ability to define problems

"Be able to assimilate relevant data

"Conceptualize information and reorganize it

"Make inductive and deductive leaps with it

"Ask hard questions

"Discuss their findings with colleagues

"Work collaboratively to find solutions

"Convince others of their position

"You know, the ability to communicate and integrate ideas, not just react to directions."

"Well, I appreciate the problem, but I don't know what we can do about it. We're not a job training center. The government sponsors community programs that do that. Our role as an institution of higher learning is to expand the minds of our students, enabling them to pursue endeavors of their choice."

Leonard frowned and said, "Well, I hadn't put it in those words, but wouldn't you agree that the university has at least two roles? One is the expansion of knowledge and the other preparing people for life. When we send Bruce to college won't that be part of what we'll be paying for? To most of us, that means his being able to get a job. For us at Terra, we need people with technical degrees and that number is declining."

"Whether the numbers are declining or not depends on if you count all graduates or just American citizens."

"What? How many non-Americans are there?"

"About half; it's a huge, national, issue. In recent years there's been a huge decline in the number of American-born students pursuing higher degrees in the technical, math, and science areas. At the same time, there's been a big jump in the number of foreign-born students pursuing science, technical, and math degrees in our schools. At this point, the foreign students account for about half of all those who graduate."

"Even at Chantilly?"

"Yes. We're very popular with Central and South American, Indian, and Far Eastern students. For example, we've already accepted McKenzie's Isabel into our Waste Water Engineering program."

"Isabel?"

Chapter 9

"A Central American girl McKenzie sponsored from K through 12. When her student visa goes through, she'll be living with McKenzie. And if we didn't have students like Isabel, we'd have to close some of our programs."

"Oh, yeah, the President of the Chamber, Ted Bruer, said something about her. Can McKenzie afford that?"

"Oh, no. Her village is paying for it."

"So, half of your technical degrees go to non-U.S. students?"

Maureen replied, "That's right, and most of them are here on student visas and go home when they graduate. That doesn't leave very many Americans, and that's bound to impact your workforce, unless you hire non-U.S."

"Well, that's sometimes *possible* for us, and for some other industries, but the government and my colleagues in defense *can't* hire non-U.S. for security reasons.

"Anyway, thank you for returning my call, Maureen. You've been very helpful."

"Anytime, Leonard. Say hi to Alice for me."

Leonard closed the connection, and sat there for a moment considering. Terra's workforce problem was becoming clearer, but he still didn't see a pattern to the data. He decided to talk with George, get his views, and find out more about those Lyceum ambassadors.

As she walked through the Chronicle's office, McKenzie noted the deepening frown lines on Bill in Circulation, and the defeated droop of Jason's shoulders in Advertising Sales. They'd been acting like the last mice in a boa constrictor's cage, and rumors had been growing for weeks.

Her purse plopped onto her desk next to a series of photos of a dark haired, olive complexioned, girl.

McKenzie sat in her chair, stared at the photos while her computer booted up, and smiled. The most faded photo showed a grubby, big-eyed little girl who looked about four, but had actually been five. The next showed the same girl, taller and healthier, and smiling at the camera. The smile broadened as the girl grew, from gap-toothed pre-adolescent to early teen. The last photo revealed a proud young woman standing in front of a mud-brick schoolhouse, and was signed, "Dear Auntie Jordan, Thank you for everything! All my love, Isabel."

She grabbed the latest edition of the Chronicle out of her "in" box, flipped through it to the society section, and scanned the article on George's party. It was topped with a 2-column photo of George being backslapped and glad-handed by the crowd—taken while she and Leonard were arguing. No mention of that, of course, just the usual happy events and smiling faces.

When her computer finished beeping, McKenzie opened Act©, checked her notes on Jane Dawson, grabbed the paper again, and scanned the sports section. Then she put on her earphone, autodialed Terra Waste Management and said, "Extension 201 please."

...

"Jane. This is McKenzie, how is everyone?"

...

"Fifteen! He must be growing like a weed, has he made the team yet?"

...

"I'll bet he makes first string next year."

...

"I have a couple tickets nobody's using to Saturday's Cougars game, first row, right on the free-throw line. I'll bet Jake would love."

...

"Birthday present from me. Shall I messenger them?

Chapter 9

...

"To your house. Right. I'm sure they'll enjoy it."

...

"Say, Jane, the reason I called, he finally OK'd an interview."

...

"Monday."

...

"10:00 AM would be fine. I'll see you then."

McKenzie hung up, updated her notes on Jane and her family, and arranged for two of the Chronicle's tickets to be delivered to the Dawson residence. Then she stood, and went to see her Editor.

McKenzie sauntered into Anna's office and flipped a business card onto her desk.

"What's this?" asked Anna. She scooped it up, glanced at it and said, "Leonard Allegren! He gave you his card?"

McKenzie grinned and said, "With an invitation to a personal meeting."

"How'd you pull that off?" demanded Anna.

"We talked after the Lyceum meeting."

"He was there?"

"Joined up."

"Leonard Allegren *joined* something?"

"Yup."

"Why."

"Houston and S.J. argued about education. Houston brought up some statistics. Superintendent Brode pushed back with her own. S.J. weighed in. They were all over the place. Same numbers, different results."

"Leonard was visiting, sitting in the back with Ted Bruer, to see George installed. But he jumped right in, said they had the same problem at Terra, and outlined how they'd handle it."

"In front of witnesses. Did you get it down?"

"Anna, you know we can't print details from Lyceum meetings. They'd kick me out, and I'd lose all those sources."

Anna sighed dramatically and said, "Yeah, yeah. OK, but you see what it tells us about Terra?"

"They're having recruitment *and* education problems."

"And that," said Anna, "makes lots of sense. I've been talking with some of my editor friends—"

"Editors have friends?"

"—at local papers across the country, and they've been hearing similar stories, from businesses everywhere."

"Everywhere?"

"Everywhere. This is big, McKenzie, Pulitzer big, so stay on it!

Chapter 10

Defining the Problem

"Remember your Pooh Bear! I think my favorite Pooh story is '*Pooh Goes Visiting*' by A.A. Milne. Pooh goes down in Rabbit's hole and snacks on honey. As a result he has difficulty getting out again and gets stuck in the portal.

"'The fact is,' said Rabbit, 'you're stuck.'

"'It all comes,' said Pooh crossly, 'of not having front doors big enough.'

"'It all comes,' said Rabbit sternly, 'of eating too much.'

"Americans are so much like Pooh. First, we get ourselves into messes. Then, we attribute the mess we're in to the wrong thing. So we apply the wrong remedy and wonder that it doesn't work. It's important to identify all the possible precursors (social, educational, etc circumstances) to a situation (such as a lack of skills in young folk), which you have done in this book. Equally important is analysis of the robustness of the causal relationships; that is, ask continually if this potential factor has any *logical, verified* causal relationship to the situation."

Mary Bell Lockhart, Alpine, TX

Seeking the Soul of Commerce

Chapter 10

George banged the gavel and said, "Welcome to the annual Lyceum ambassadors orientation lunch." Leonard and McKenzie were sitting together in the back, which surprised those who remembered the words they exchanged at George's party. A slide projector near the front was pointed at a screen behind the President's table, and a large stranger, bald and gray-bearded, was seated at the table next to Trevor.

"It's my pleasure to announce and congratulate this year's ambassadors. You play an important role in the future of our community, as you represent all of us to other parts of the United States and the world.

"Today's speaker continues our focus on the workforce and education crisis in Chantilly. Last month Dr Edra Brode, our superintendent of schools, and Houston Campbell, a long time community member, cattle rancher, and businessman, gave us their perspectives on 'drop out rates'. Today's keynote speaker is an old friend of mine who will help us understand the source of the crisis, why it's not just an education crisis but the effect of a profound cultural evolution that is occurring right here and now. His name is Dr Stephen Glenn.

"Dr. Glenn is a transformational psychologist from Utah. Since 1967, he's been part of a national organization of individuals and groups—commissioned by Presidents Johnson, Nixon, Reagan, and Carter—to understand the changes occurring in American youth since the end of World War II. This work was prompted by the statistical decline in performance metrics of high school graduating classes that began in 1963. Dr. Glenn's perspective is relevant to our understanding of the current educational crisis, as very little has changed since he retired. He will help our ambassadors put what they learn into a historical and developmental perspective as they visit other communities.

"Please join me in giving a warm welcome to Dr. Glenn."[1]

The Lyceum members clapped politely as a large, heavyset, jovial man stepped up to the podium. Immediately likeable, the applause grew louder momentarily, and then faded as he waved the crowd to silence. Dr. Glenn picked up a remote control unit, tethered to the slide projector, and pushed a button.

Ted closed the blind and dimmed the lights, and Dr Glenn said, "The fifty years after World War II were the most turbulent in human history, and to help us understand where we are today, how we got here, and where we have to go for a better set of alternatives for our future, I'm going to summarize how those years have impacted family, schools, and young people.

"In an attempt to avoid being lengthy and incredible, I would like to use a series of pictures to show you where we appear to be with this generation of young people, the primary factors that have put us there, and what appear to be our most exciting and reliable strategies for moving on to a more productive future.

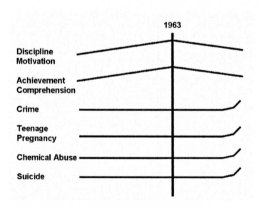

"These top lines here chart the performance of high school seniors, every year, for the

---

[1] The following contains the transcript of a lecture by Dr. Stephen Glenn, and is used here with permission. See the Bibliography for details.

20th century. As you can see, from 1900 to 1963 every group of young people to arrive at 17 got there stronger in discipline and motivation, stronger in achievement and comprehension, than the group ahead of them, and infinitely superior to their parents. And on January 1st 1963 that whole pattern reversed itself, and for the next 20 years, with no exceptions, went steadily in the opposite direction."

Houston's thoughts turned to his granddaughter. He wondered if and how this affected her, as Dr. Glenn said, "For a while we blamed this on urbanization, technology, and future shock. But then we were faced with the fact that many other highly urbanized, highly advanced nations were not having that experience, and were beginning to come up to equal and in some cases go past us. That caused us to think a little more thoughtfully about the rather pat suggestions we were given in the 60s that this is the way it should be.

"At the exact moment that this downward trend began, look at the bottom." Raising his right hand and ticking off each point by tapping a finger on his thumb, Dr. Glen said, "Notice that crime, teenage pregnancy, drug and alcohol abuse, and teenage suicide had remained stable at low levels through two major world wars, through a massive depression, and through the only true nuclear holocaust of our lifetime. None of those rocked this boat significantly.

"But the very year that conditions that should have supported achievement appeared to weaken, the bottom began to rise to fill that vacuum, suggesting, of course, that those are reciprocal curves and that factors that are producing one may in fact be producing all; and we know that to be true today. Notice, if you will, that for the next twenty years as achievement slid, crime, teenage pregnancy, drug and alcohol abuse, and teenage suicide rose at about the same equal rate. Then the exact year that America responded to the 'Nation at Risk' report by allowing forty states to make a wholesale rush toward quantity rather than the more costly element of quality—" waving a pointed finger in time to each point, Dr. Glenn said, "by demanding more hours, more accountability, more tests, and more pressure, without any change in class size, teaching methods, or so on—we drove the pressure upward, but in the wrong direction."

Clay Collins, the Principal of Chantilly High, nodded in agreement, as Dr. Glenn continued with, "What we have today is, the survivors have looked a little stronger on paper, but we have the highest drop out rate we've ever had. The marginal kids are dropping out in increased numbers, and the kids already frustrated by the process have shown a greater tendency toward suicide, sexual acting out, drug abuse, and so on. You can really see those little skis on the end if you realize that the Baby Boom ended in 65 and the number of babies dropped by 25% at that moment.

"From 1965 to 75 the number of children diminished by 25%. From 1975 to 1985 the number of teenagers dropped by 25%. If we'd stayed at the same level we were at in numbers of suicides per thousand, numbers of babies per thousand, adolescents, and so on, then we should have had this morning 25% fewer of all of those because we have 25% fewer young people. But instead, when we woke this morning, we had 25% more of all of those, and that's a much more serious problem." S.J. frowned and nodded as she realized that that was when the nation began to see another large increase in immigrants, prayer taken out of schools, televisions in homes, marketing directly to consumers, and credit cards.

Dr. Glenn said, "What it suggests is that if you demand achievement and productivity without developing the necessary skills to deliver it, then you will increasingly drive more and more people out of the system and into more destructive areas of their life. If the nation demands more of its young people, we have to look at how strong their toolboxes are to carry them across that threshold, and we have to be very, very careful that we don't put that pressure on in a bankrupt system as we've been doing. Until we deal with the underlying pressure, what we tend to do is make the ones next to it worse for a while.

"But the exciting piece is, left on their own, 99% of all human beings, from birth, seek as their most desired path in life to earn the recognition of positive people around them who they want to look up to them or respect their achievements and accomplishments.

"When conditions frustrate that, then it will go outward sideways. Better to be important in a gang then insignificant altogether; better to trade off my body as a commodity than to be totally overlooked altogether; better to disrupt a class than to be invisible in it because I'm not strong academically. People will find other ways to express that need for recognition." ...

Everyone in the hall, parents, business people, administrators, began to resonate with the speech.

"Overall, we know today what we're looking at here, in individual lives and in the culture, is very much like a waterbed mattress with too much pressure in it. We suddenly filled the mattress too full with pressure, and everywhere the rubber is weak it bulged. If we pressed on the individual bulges without relieving the pressure inside, it would just affect everything else temporarily, come right back, and a million bulge prevention programs would fail until you found the valve and started to regulate the pressure. But once you are working at the valve, activities that had no apparent relationship to the bulges might do more to resolve them than all the bulge specific programs we could ever come up with.

"That's what took us so long to find it. America was so preoccupied with bulges we never looked thoughtfully at the pressure. It was not until 1981 that we even went out and consciously gathered up our successful young people, to study them in the same detail we'd been studying the failures for 20 years. But the first step in solving an epidemic is to find out how your survivors differ from those who are caught up in it. And we hadn't taken that step.

"In '81 we began to develop a detailed list, an analysis of the many thousands of young people born in the worst ghettoes in this country, many who lived in homes of ten children, of all different ages and all different fathers, with a mother who was herself a third generation welfare recipient, surrounded by rats, hookers, pimps, pushers, going to drug infested, violence prone overcrowded schools, who got all ten of those kids out of there without one getting arrested, without one being treated for anything, didn't have one drop out of school, and not one of those kids today is not substantially more successful than their mother was. And did it with every strike in the book against her, alongside parents who lost ten out of ten in the same environment.

"And when we began to look thoughtfully at that, we found it was what was not happening to our young people in certain areas of skill development, rather than what was happening to them in the environment, that determined the outcome. And that opened a whole new world of options for us as people.

Dr. Glenn waved an arm, as he said, "We then asked, 'what happened to a whole culture to cause such a dramatic change?' A 180° reversal in one year suggests something cataclysmic happened to the culture.

114

We tried to blame it on the 60s for a many years, and that's why we didn't find it—it's naïve to assume that a 17 year old is a product of the year they turned 17. But if you recognize you're looking at a 17-year cumulative journey through a force field of relationships and institutions, then go back to the year those kids were born, draw a line, and begin to study the force field they're passing through, that's when you find major elements that change on a wide scale. Then put that in the hopper, and soon you'll have a list of the things they've been through and what you have to compensate for."

Recognizing the process, Leonard nodded in agreement and sucked thoughtfully on his lower lip and considered the effects on Bruce.

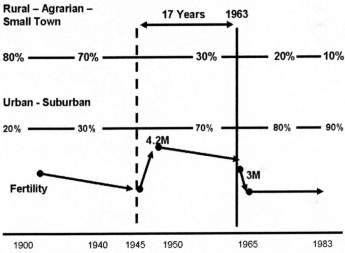

Dr. Glenn clicked on the remote, a second graphic appeared and he said, "We struck pay dirt when we went back 17 years from 1963, when the problem first appeared in high school seniors. It's a group of children born in 1946; but notice the environment.

"According to the census of 1940, 70% of America

was rural, agrarian, small town nation. But 10 years later we were exactly 70% urban-suburban. That's a 180° reversal in our lifestyle in ten years. Europe took 350 years to do this, Japan took 1000 years to do it, and no one moved anywhere, they just emerged and adapted.

"We essentially sent in excess of six million young men away to fight World War II, most of them from rural, agrarian, small town America. They got committed to the war when it was discovered that war had changed. More than any other war in history, technology was determining the outcome, and the Germans were ahead of us in innovation. We had one hope, to out produce them. But how could we out produce them with our manpower gone?

"Up until then, 'woman power' meant school teachers, secretarial help, nurses, and garment workers. Everybody knew a woman couldn't weld, rivet, design, supervise, test pilot, or truck drive, but all of a sudden they were all the world had. In one year five million young women left the farms and villages they'd grown up in, went into the defense plants, took on a 40 hour work week, temporary housing, daycare for their children, the attractiveness of wages, and showed the whole world that they *could* weld, rivet, design, supervise, test pilot, truck drive, well enough to save the world from the Nazis.

"But when the war ended, those women faced the greatest existential crisis of their life; 'Do we go back to the world we came from and shut down all these opportunities, or do we take the risks of trying a new lifestyle, and attempt to secure for our children the things we did without ourselves." McKenzie nodded in understanding, recalling her grandmother's stories about what she had gone through.

Dr. Glen snatched up the microphone, stepped back,

Chapter 10

and pointed to the image on the screen, as he said, "At the same moment, the young men coming home from war had, like the young women, just been through a depression and the rationing of war time, and associated their rural home with great material insecurity and a major shortage of opportunity. So these men and women came together and six million couples were formed in one twelve month period of time from middle '45 to middle '46, and five million more joined them in the next 12 months. An incredible *11 million* new couples asking, 'Where do we go for our lives?' in that two year interval.

"Most of them did what parents have done since the beginning of time. They decided to try to make abundant for their children that which was in shortest supply as they grew up, and then did what parents have done forever—they lived to criticize their own children for not appreciating all the things they made abundant."

The Lyceum members laughed, appreciatively. Dr. Glenn paused while they did so and then said, "But this group of young parents was faced with new obstacles. Historically, a young couple wanting to change their life condition would marry, have their children, raise them into early adolescence—surrounded by grandmas, grandpas, aunts, uncles, nieces, nephews, in a lifestyle the parents were already used to—until they'd saved up enough money to buy a small piece of land down the road a few miles, and that was the break away. But this year, the G.I. Bill became available, and 11 million couples, just by fantasizing it, grabbed the brass ring of opportunity and set out on a whole new frontier.

"But their dream was, 'If we can provide everything for these children, and spare them any contact with the realities of a hard life, somehow these kids will emerge strong, confident, effective, successful human beings,' and there began the seeds of our downfall—that assumption.

"We know today that the number one best way to destroy self-concept, self-esteem, motivation, and initiative is to do too much for a person, and the second best strategy is to give them too much generic praise—'you're great, you're terrific, you're wonderful'—without any base of clearly understood validation of that praise. And so, in the 60s all the problems of low self-esteem, lack of personal initiative, and insecurity, began going up dramatically. But all the cultural elements of success—confidence, self-discipline, judgment—began deteriorating. We were in trouble.

"Tragically, a whole generation of young parents who had gone without meals at the bottom of the depression, without everything they basically wanted in wartime, now decided that they should both work 24 hours a day, if necessary, to surround their children with such an abundance of food that the child never had to consider where it came from or if it would be available, believing this should produce in their children a very deep, passionate appreciation for fast food."

Dr. Glenn paused while the Lyceum laughed again, then continued with, "A whole generation of parents— who had been barefoot at the bottom of the depression, and in the rationing of wartime, had probably had worn-out shoes they stuffed with cardboard to keep going— now believed they should create for each child, at no cost to the child in time and effort, their own closet filled with the exact shoe for each event or activity, including the designer monogram most cherished at the moment, believing that that would produce in their children a deep, fundamental respect for Nike®, Adidas®, and Reebok®.

"A whole generation of parents, who themselves had been grateful for hand-me-downs at the bottom of the depression, and had probably shown each other, in wartime, clothing they'd just made from flour sacks, sugar bags, and old draperies, decided they should create for each child their own closet with the exact costume for each event or activity, including the monogram of whoever they were rooting for that weekend, believing this should always produce in their children a very deep respect and appreciation for Gloria Vanderbilt®, Calvin Klein®, and Guess®. There was a time in America when children wore jeans because parents were poor. But today parents are poor because children wear jeans."

The hall laughed again and Dr. Glenn continued, saying, "In *Fires of Spring*, Michener said, 'There are two great tragedies in our life. One is to lose our life's dream, but the other is to get it too early or too easily, so that you have nothing to validate yourself or your journey through life by.'[2] That became an important challenge, because last year 91% of all adolescents who took their own life took it because they perceived they were not an asset or a contributor to themselves or anyone else, but a burden.

"We also found that if we set up clinics and passed out contraceptives in every high school and junior high in the country, we'd reduce abortions and venereal disease, but no more than 25% of the births. Seventy-five to 80% of the babies born were a clear decision, conscious or subconscious, by a young woman to create a condition in her life that gave her meaning, purpose, significance, status, something that needed her, that she was an asset to, that she didn't have to prove anything to. Their alternative is being told 'keep your

---

[2] The actual quote appears to be from Dr. Jonas Salk, the inventor of the Polio Vaccine: "There are two great tragedies in life. One is to not get what you want; the other is to get what you want. And if I had gotten what I wanted, it would have been a greater tragedy than my not getting what I wanted, because it allowed me to get something else."

mouth shut, keep out of difficulty, do what we tell you, appreciate what we do for you,' or to have people say, 'you're a woman now; you have something that needs you, you're important, you're an asset to something,' and that's very significant.

"We've found that young people who don't contribute significant things in each class, each week, stop valuing the process, become resistant to it, and drop away. And yet we found that what the Baby Boom did was create an education model in which students have become passive scribes, sitting down and recording the teacher's contribution.

"Previously, in a one-room school house, the teacher called them up and validated them. The average class had kids ten years apart in age and readiness, and older students prepared the lessons for younger. So if a child was home sick, the lesson wasn't taught because the kid had the lesson, not the teacher. Not all six year olds had to learn the same thing at the same time, because the teacher was used to working with individual children.

"You see the word 'to teach' in Latin means to draw forth, or 'to bring out through dialogue,' understanding. Putting the data in is where the teaching should start. Drawing out the understanding was the real teaching process, and for centuries that's how it was done. But suddenly what happened?

"The birth rate had been declining for a half century. People moved to the city slowly, found they now

Characteristics of Successful Individuals

1. <u>Strong</u> Perception of Personal Capabilities
2. <u>Strong</u> Perception of Personal Significance
3. <u>Strong</u> Perception of Personal Power/Influence
4. <u>Strong</u> Intra-personal Skills
5. <u>Strong</u> Inter-personal Skills
6. <u>Strong</u> Systemic Skills
7. <u>Strong</u> Judgmental Skills

Chapter 10

worked 50 hours a week, away from their home, for low pay, had no place to put children, nothing for them to do, no one to help raise them, and they were incredibly expensive. It made less and less sense to have them in large numbers, so they quit. The census of 1940 showed that 37% of the fertile couples lived in the city, had only 8% of the babies born that year, and described themselves as the largest group of single-child and childless couples ever seen in the country's history.

"Meanwhile, in the rural and small town world where you needed children in your economic life—they were a very necessary asset, you had a network to help raise them, a role for them to play, a safe place for them to grow up, and you could afford them—the average couple there had five, and that's the way we came out of this.

"But those first 11 million couples, rushed right out to have five children as fast as they could, before we even asked, 'where will we put them, who will raise them, what role will they play, is anything ready?' and touched off a major emergency.

"History shows that a vast army of children was born in 1946, and lived exactly five years before it dawned on anyone in America that they would one day go to school."

The group laughed again and then Dr. Glenn said, "Suddenly, on September 1st, 1951, with no advanced warning, eight times the usual number of first graders arrived in five minutes, looking for a seat. And people said 'Where did you come from?' and the kids said, 'I've been around for five years, I thought you saw me coming,' and we hadn't.

"Class size jumped. The class of 62 never sat in a class larger than 20, but the class of 63 never had a class smaller than 35. So every hour in the classroom there was 50% more competition for time, attention, encouragement, contribution; and education became too passive to develop critical thinking, moral and ethical development, encouragement, commitment, growth, and so that first group of kids—although they were a whole peer group of first-borns,· who generally knock the top off in achievement—were overcrowded from the beginning and started downhill.

"Have you ever heard somebody say, 'American children are forced to mature earlier'? Do you believe it? We always mistake sophistication for maturity. It's absolutely true that we have school kids who have observed more bizarre acts of human sexuality by the age of seven than their grandparents fantasized in an entire lifetime. But, there's no evidence that those children are maturing anywhere near the same rate in self-discipline, judgment, responsibility, clarity on the nature of life, and in their role in it, than the people ahead of them did. In fact, the last set of studies shows it now takes 16 years to achieve, in these areas, in an American child, what was once normal at 11. It takes until 26 to achieve an 18-year level, against the norms of the 50s. And if you really want to destroy lives, create a gap between sophistication and maturity in favor of sophistication."

Martha Fleming struggled with what she was hearing. Her son Ryan was this year's Chantilly High valedictorian. He and his friends seemed to have done just fine, had been accepted to fine colleges and universities, and yet what Dr. Glenn was saying was very troubling.

Dr. Glenn continued, saying, "The group most at risk to this gap is the group who starts puberty at about 11. Fertility starts three years earlier now than for children at the turn of the 20th century. The enormous increase in latchkey children this age, the lack of networks, families moving every 2½ years on average—even close friends you've known for a while are not there most of the time—and so last year the average age at which American children start to get drunk was 11 ½, and by age 13 one out of every three is sexually active to some degree, with their first sexual encounter coming during the 12th year of their life, in an unattended family home while drinking beer or wine available to them in that home.

"But look at what happened in addition to all these changes, at the same moment. We once rode to every major event in our lives in wagons that moved slowly and were filled with discussion. Boredom alone encouraged conversation between family members. But today we've created metal cylinders that fly down freeways, are filled with CD players, FM radios, DVD players, Gameboys®, Cells, and iPods®. So now it's possible to go all the way from here to St. Louis and never say more than, 'Are you sure you have to go *now*?'

The Lyceum laughed and Dr. Glenn said, "That's a very difficult world in which to feel close, affirmed, and influenced. I think John Nesbit said it very well, when he said, 'When we immersed ourselves in a hi-tech lifestyle, we began to starve to death visibly in all areas that required personal affirmation.' Spouses began to lose their connections, children and parents became polarized, teacher and student relationship deteriorated, and employer-employee relationships became more stressful.

"Human beings never feel close, develop trust, and are not influenced by the thinking of people they don't believe listen to them. It requires 'dialogue,' 'a meaningful exchange of perceptions in a climate of support or interest in my responses.' Numbers drove dialogue out of the classroom in 1951, and technology drove it out of the family at about that time.

"Many American families will go home, and with all the challenges to our influence on each other, will slip into the pattern of, 'Did you have a good day?' 'Did that work out for you?' 'Are you all right?'

"Watch how many times today people say, 'Did you, can you, do you, will you, won't you, aren't you,' to each other. Because, you see, 'Did you, can you, do you, will you, won't you, aren't you,' can all be answered with a harrumph, shrug, grunt, or nothing. And we're grunting ourselves right out of our future. You see, when I say, 'Did you, can you, do you, will you, won't you, aren't you,' I'm reducing you to a multiple choice, true or false, stimulus response item. I'm carefully limiting my exposure to thoughts, ideas, and beliefs. Most of the time I'm going to decide what I'm willing to let you experience and you can grunt either way.

"We do this most with children, when we can least afford to. We assume little children don't have much insight, and instead of recognizing that they never will until their parents and teachers encourage through dialogue their thoughts and ideas, we reduce them to, 'Did you have fun?' instead of, 'What things were fun for you?' 'Did you like that picture?' instead of, 'What things do you enjoy in that picture?'

"According to the National Assessment Project, American children show no growth whatsoever in the ability to organize thoughts and ideas, interact with concepts, formulate and express meaningful insight, after they leave the sixth grade. Whatever they have in the sixth grade is all they will have in the 12th grade, and they traced that to the tendency of teachers to use objective tests exclusively, which are easier to grade and administer, at the exact time that kids need dialogue, case studies, essay exams, and interaction with ideas.

"They traced it to a heavy reliance to correcting grammar or data rather than engaging in significant dialogue about the organization, implications, and al-

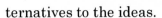

ternatives to the ideas.

"They traced it to a tendency on the part of parents and teachers generally to face puberty—where kids often become fairly inarticulate about their new experience—with 'why can't you ever, how come you never, surely you realize, how many times do I have to tell you, when are you going to, you know better than that!' and kids very quickly learn that the last thing on earth people want is their thoughtful response. And soon they start to say, 'I don't know,' and grunt and shrug, and you start to say, 'Did you, can you, do you, will you, won't you, aren't you,' and we die right there.

"And Don Dewar pointed out that as soon as we replace that passive 'You know what we want, someone else will do it if you don't' in the workplace, with Key Management, Quality Circles, where people feel listened to, taken seriously, and significant, we get productivity, loyalty, low turnover, reduction in stress, across the board, but you had to have dialogue to do it.

"I came into my hotel the other day, turned on ESPN, and there was a tractor pull. You'll watch anything when you're on the road, and so I'm watching it diligently, and the announcer was announcing away, and suddenly he saw these beautiful young people. And I'm sure a thought went through him 'I'd like to involve them in my show.' You know how he did it?

"'Were you scared when that tractor blew up?' 'Powerful things aren't they?' 'Great to be here isn't it?' right down the line. Three grunts, four shrugs, and one indeterminate gesture, and it was over.

"Next day I turned on the Today Show® and there was an eminent weather man, and he had four young women who had allegedly won an award for intelligence, but we'll never know because he didn't say, 'What do you believe will be the most important thing that happens in your life because of this?' 'What were the special things you had to do to be worthy of this honor?' Instead, it was, 'Great to be here isn't it?' 'Bet you're excited about this aren't ya?" three grunts, two shrugs, one gesture, and it was over for them.

"And in fact, watch how many times this week you, who are aware and care, or those you come in contact with, will say, 'How are you?' and then not stop to find out. Have you seen that? It's kind of the ultimate rip off.

"'How are you?' and you just turn to deal with the attention and they're gone, there's the back of their head. They didn't care!

"So one thing we've been doing all week is telling everybody, thousands of us last week committed to tell everybody who said, 'How are yah?' exactly how we were in extensive detail. I've already told 50 people this week who didn't care, in great detail, exactly how I was.

"Yesterday I got on the elevator at the 15th floor of the Mariotte Hotel A. man stepped on and said, "How are you?' and I said, 'Oh, thank God you asked me. I'm a long way from home, real concerned about this terror situation, my airlines cancelled...' By the time we got to the fifth floor he's in a corner like this and I said, 'Sir, sir, you're visibly uncomfortable.' And he said, 'Darn right I am.' And I said, 'Well, I just wanted to make the point that out here on the road there are a lot of us lonely, chemically dependent, suicidal individuals who believe that no one cares, and you shouldn't raise false hopes. And he said, 'I won't, I won't!'

"'Now listen, 'How are you?' should only be asked with eye contact and genuine openness to my thoughts. If you don't want to know, don't ask.' If you and I had got on here and gone 'Ugh' and looked at the numbers, we would have made it.

"But, as it turns out, I was human and you say

essentially 'what is significant in your life this morning?' and when I start to tell you to back off, that's real painful man. Real painful. He said 'I'm going to remember this as long as I live!'

"By then we hit the ground floor, the doors opened, and he started to leave. I grabbed him and said, 'And by the way, how are you?' and he said, 'Real freaked out by this!'

"But at least I got his thoughtful response, and I know its true because he left his briefcase, so I picked it up to take it to him. He thought I wanted to go on telling him how I was, so he was running by the time he got to the door. So I sent it out with the Bellman. But I don't think he'll rip off so many people this week.

"And if you think it's frivolous, just let me come back and say, 'The language of love and respect in the classroom and home consists of 'what did you, where did you, when did you, how did you, what was your understanding of, let me be sure I understand,' and a moment to validate that. And it's surprising we have to spend three full days intensively retraining professional teachers to break the habit of 'can any of you think of an example?' let's everybody look down and wait until the teacher does it, and begin to again build confidence in this one critical process. But if you checked it off, can anyone here in this room ever develop a friendship with another human being without a meaningful exchange of perception in a climate of support or interest; which is what 'dialogue' means?

"When we court, we spend hours and hours in dialogue, act incredibly interested, and create something beautiful called 'love.' If we're not careful we marry, cut out the dialogue, substitute expectations, begin to do business together and ruin the relationship. Have you seen that happen to your neighbors?"

Laughter, followed by, "But if you ever want to get back the love, what's the one ingredient you have to put back in to find it? Dialogue. And if you don't increase that basic dialogue, nothing will ever come back for you.

"Have you ever noticed, when a human being's life falls totally apart, or they become chemically dependent and we detoxify them, the only way we can heal them and have them grow is to dialogue with them? Until we listen to you, consider and invite your thoughts and ideas without discounting you, and work with you as an asset in your life, no healing will ever occur. So this year we'll spend billions of dollars hiring professional therapists to do what we could have done voluntarily in homes and classrooms, and taught kids to do with each other.

- The Absence of Networks
- The Absence of Meaningful Roles
- The Absence of On the Job Training
- The Absence of Parenting Resources

"As a result of all the changes we've been through, we've made a major shift from overtly supportive education, parenting, and young people, to non-supportive. And as each of those changed we became, for the first time in this nation's history, the first generation of Americans who tried to raise and educate a whole generation of children without any active support from networks of grandmas, grandpas, aunts, uncles, nieces, nephews, neighbors, in-laws, and friends to share the experience and work together.

"We became so isolated that in the '60s, fewer than 2 million Americans in a whole year gave any time to self-help groups, neighborhood initiatives, or volunteerism. And that was the exact moment the screams for help of a young woman in New York City went unattended, and 38 people rationalized their refusal to save her life by saying it was her problem, not theirs. That's as isolated as Americans ever became.

"Today in part through the Lions, Lyceum, and other groups, this week alone 49 million Americans will give some time to self-help programs, community school initiatives, Big Brothers, Big Sisters, safe rides programs, and safe homes programs. We can't overlook the impact. We've done more with dialogue and collaboration among neighbors, in the form of Neighborhood Crime Watches, to curtail urban crime than we got in billions of dollars in thirty years of federal and state effort that couldn't work until people reached out and began to do things together.

"You and I are the first generation in this country's history to try to raise a whole generation of children whose toolboxes for the journey of life were being filled by part-time contributions of one or two inexperienced biological relatives, rather than the collective contribution of networks of parents, teachers, and neighbors who knew each other intimately, worked together extensively over a long period of time, and in many cases offered an apprenticeship in many of the realities of life.

"The skills of life were inadvertently suppressed, and once those are suppressed, everything we dream of is out of reach, and everything that strikes us as horrifying is most likely to creep in. So we found we were the first who ever had to thoughtfully identify the skills our young people would need and ask thoughtfully how they would be transmitted in our homes and classrooms.

"These are the first generations of young people in this country's history whose on the job training for life comes more from exposure to the media than from hands-on involvement with the learning, and achieving, and managing necessary to provide for their needs, and we have to be very careful with this. If we put young people in little homes, in the suburbs or in the city, and then parents go away to provide lifestyles for those children, inadvertently the child's perceptions become 'parents go away and get money' and when they come home your job is to hassle, manipulate, and wish, and if you do that well you go first class.

"And parents reinforce that. Dad comes home and says 'plain pocket jeans' and the kids pitch a fit, threaten to drop out of school, and go away in designer jeans. Mom comes home and says 'department store shoes' and the kids threaten terminal social ostracism, and go away in Reeboks® or something. But the kids are never there when dad passes up lunch to provide the better jeans, and never there when mom dyes her shoes instead of replacing them, so the kids get the best of everything. And a whole generation of young people comes up to the threshold of puberty believing that if they just hassle, manipulate, and wish, things will work out in their favor. And when they try that chemically, sexually, socially, legally, we end up where we did last year. 55,000 12 to 21 year olds died between January 1st and December 31st last year without one natural death.

"Isn't that awesome?

"56,000 died in five years in Vietnam, but stinking thinking killed 55,000 last year at home. We had 280,000 permanently impaired in five years in Vietnam; we had 350,000 12 to 21 year olds impaired in the last twelve months. 20,000 deaths due to accidents, and over 100,000 permanent impairments, and ¾ of those accidents were drug and alcohol related, 7,200 suicides, most of them due to lack of perception of meaning and purpose.

"This is the first time we've ever *had* to ask, 'What is necessary for children to discover their significance in their own life?'

"Now, the most important thing I can say to conclude is, the young person most likely to fall short of their potential, and most likely to show up as a casualty, is being raised and educated in family and school systems that have *not* adapted to the new social challenges. And, the young person most likely to achieve their potential, to succeed in life, are those who are being allowed to accumulate the belief, experience, the understanding, that '*I am a capable person* who can initiate learning and thinking when I need to,' and to realize that, 'My life is significant, *I matter.*'

Characteristics of High Risk Individuals

1. Weak Perception of Personal Capabilities
2. Weak Perception of Personal Significance
3. Weak Perception of Personal Power/Influence
4. Weak Intra-personal Skills
5. Weak Inter-personal Skills
6. Weak Systemic Skills
7. Weak Judgmental Skills

"A high risk individual today is being raised and educated by parents and teachers who have found it easier to take care of them and criticize them than to help them encounter the impact they have over their life. If I run down and deliver lunches to my child, and the child is good at forgetting things, that's the worst mistake I could make. The loving parent would wean them of their irresponsibility. When a child says 'I've left my lunch home' a wise mother today says in her heart, 'Is this a pattern?' If the answer is 'No, this kid is usually responsible about everything, but was a little rushed today getting that project on the bus,' then you drop it off. But if you say, 'Is this a repeating pattern? Yes, forgotten gym shorts, forgotten lunches.' Then you must love the child enough to say, 'Listen Dear, thanks for telling me about your lunch. I'll put it in the refrigerator right now so it won't spoil. You have a great day. See you tonight.' Hang up with dignity and let them work it out.

"I had a mother rush up to me and say, 'I'm a single parent due to divorce. I work all day on one job, all night on another. I stop off at home to cook for my nineteen year old son. My problem is I can't get him to cook, can't get him to take the initiative, what do I do?'

"I said, 'Take this quarter, go over to the phone, call him and say, I just met someone interesting, I'm going to dinner with him. And hang up. She said, 'what will happen?' I said, 'Frankly I don't know, but I have observed 19 year olds become incredibly self reliant when confronted with their own starvation. (Laughter)

"Okay...I observed one once who ate raw bread. I heard of another who was caught eating Spaghetti O's® cold. It's incredible what they can do if left on their own. Remember, I'm not talking about neglect, only weaning. And remember that weaning has never been attractive to the weanor or the weanee. (Laughter)

"But it's always been essential to their survival. And you know the first thing we have to do to treat a chemically dependent kid? We have to get others to quit taking responsibility for them, and let them encounter their influence over their life, so they can stop pretending they're a victim of others, and begin to face their own collusion in what happens to them. And the earlier that lesson is taught the better off we will be. If you replace a little dose of patience, self-discipline, and insight about my affect on my life when I'm young, I don't self-destruct so quickly in puberty.

"Then I have to have skills. If you encourage self-assessment, self-control, and let me encounter the difference between the jeans I want and the jeans that are reasonable for my family, is some setting aside of what I want in order to put forth the effort to do what I need to, then I'll have self-discipline when I need it. The more you invite a meaningful exchange of perceptions, the more skill you help me develop that which will later allow me to communicate, cooperate, negotiate, share, and comprehend effectively. And that will be an asset in relationships, education, and the job, but without it I'll fail there, for no other reason than that I don't have the skills to be effective.

"Then you have the goals of the program we're about to look at. An exciting thing is, everywhere we've been able to strengthen and increase these skills, we've gotten an incredibly exciting set of options and they were all positive in their direction. And I think history will record the finest hour of this nation was not when we brought an end to polio, was not when we put people on the moon, it was when we took the steps to stop discouraging the next generation of Salks and Churchills, and so on. We need those Jonas Salks today more than ever today to deal the next virus that's challenging us.

"But Jonas Salk said very beautifully when a reporter asked, 'How does this incredible success cause you to look back on your previous failures?' He said, 'I've never had a failure in my life. I don't understand what you're talking about. My family didn't think in those terms. We never said you blew it, you messed it up, why can't you, how come you never. My parents said, when I dropped my first jug of milk at three, Jonas, why don't you have a good look at that and see if you can find a better way to hang onto it. And now that you've got a good grip on the jug, why, see what you can think of to help me clean up the mess your first experiment made.' He said 'that taught me to try, ask what, why, and how.' He said, 'This is my 201st journey into the unknown. It would have been impossible if I'd been intimidated or ashamed by my first attempt.'

"And we need those learners today, and the skills to

develop them.

"I always admired Winston Churchill, who was raised that way. If you look at him, there was the kind of man who if we could generate those same things in this generation of kids... He had problems, he was an ugly man, but even that he faced squarely. He said, 'Someone had to make a British Bulldog look handsome by contrast.' He was an alcoholic, but he never let that get him down and worked to overcome it his whole life. Popularity wasn't an issue for him. He was rejected more for his views than anyone in modern British history. But did that intimidate him? Not at all. What was he known for in history, not his 400 literary works, not his definitive history of World War II, not his Pulitzer Prizes, but the incredible fortitude and strength of his will when it was needed, when he stood up to challenge the tide of defeatism in his countrymen who said, 'Anything's better than living in bomb shelters, let's make a deal with the Nazis.' The ugly man stood up, ignoring his lack of popularity, stuck his chin out and said, 'We'll fight them on our beaches, we'll fight them on our doorsteps, we'll fight them in our living rooms, but we'll never give in to this menace, to this tyranny.' And he galvanized the will of his people.

"He was later asked, 'Sir Winston, what in your school experience best prepared you to lead Britain out of her darkest hour?' He thought for a moment, and I'll paraphrase his response. He said, 'It was the two years I spent in the seventh grade.' (Laughter)

"Someone said, 'Did you fail?' He said, 'No, I had two opportunities to learn to do it effectively.' And he said, 'What Britain needed was not brilliance, but the will to persevere when things were going poorly, and I learned it there.'

"Another time a person said, 'Why, Sir Winston,

you're drunk!' and he said, 'Madam, you are ugly,' he said, 'but I shall be sober in the morning, and you shall still be ugly.' (Laughter)

"Okay... Let me just point out... I will just conclude by saying, our finest hour will come when we take our incredible ability to work together, to challenge the most complex environment ever seen in history, to press the frontiers of knowledge in technology farther in one person's lifetime by 500% than in the entire history of this world, into a practical model for our homes and schools of developing the skills our children need—skills for adolescence, skills for living, and cumulative skills for life. We'll only do that by networking, extending our parenting resources, carefully planning the on-the-job training, and concentrating on the tools of the learner in those toolboxes. Because this will determine where we go in the future more than anything else in our world and we need to stand up and say, 'We will fight the alternative to capable people on our beaches, in our yards, in our cities, and we'll never give into this tyranny without a fight.'

"Because you're committed to it I respect you, but for the incredible things we can accomplish if we get it together today and in the hereafters I'll only pray for God to bless each and every one of you and say, 'Thanks very much for giving this much of your morning. Thanks very much!'"

The hall applauded profusely and began standing, continuing the applause. Clay was the first to reach Dr. Glenn, before the applause died, leaned close and said, "I want to thank you! I've been the principal here for 25 years, and I've been so frustrated I was thinking of leaving. But you're dead-on, and you've given me hope."

The hall grew silent, as Clay's words became audible, but he continued, saying, "While a lot of our graduates go on to college, they've reached a... 'canyon' in their performance, and more and more of our students just stop showing up, especially during their senior year. We've been forced to put more and more emphasis on college prep classes, shifting funding away from vocational and ROP programs.

"I was so frustrated, I was considering early retirement, but you've given me new hope."

Dr. Glenn enfolded Clay's right hand in both of his and said, "I'm glad. You can make a difference," and then the hall erupted in chatter, drowning out their conversation again.

McKenzie had thoroughly enjoyed Dr. Glenn's remarks. They confirmed and added a great deal to her own research on schools, education, business, and community, and, wondering how to put the pieces together in an integrated story, she leaned toward Leonard and said, "So, Leonard, what does the businessman think about Dr. Glenn's speech?"

Caught a bit off guard, Leonard turned to her with a puzzled look on his face and asked, "What do you mean?"

She smiled and said, "Last month we talked about technology and communication, and Dr. Glenn just said a breakdown in human communication and interaction caused a fundamental change in the culture."

Leonard cocked his left brow and asked, "And?"

"Our focus was on the *technological* tools of communication, all the devices we use to communicate. Dr. Glenn focused on relationships and the interaction between generations and networks of people. The only time he mentioned technology, it was as an impediment to human interaction. I find that very interesting, particularly in light of what you're now doing at Terra, that new Omega system. You seem to focus on tools you use in your business.

Chapter 10

"I'd think you'd find the contrast interesting, between his emphasis on human skills and yours on technological tools. To an... informed... outsider like me, that seems to be one of the big issues Terra is facing right now."

"Well, as the head of Terra, one of our key issues is finding the right people, with technical knowledge and 'human skills' as you put it. That's a huge problem for us right now, and that's why I agreed to discuss it further last month."

"But do you see the difference in perspective, between interpersonal, human skills and technology?"

Leonard nodded and replied, "It reminds me of the discussion between Houston and Edra, where they used the same data to arrive at different conclusions about education. As we were listening to Dr. Glenn, the picture created in our minds was different. Why is that?"

Leonard's PDA buzzed. He whipped it out, glanced at it, put it away and said, "I've got a few minutes, care to talk?"

McKenzie smiled and nodded. Leonard waved to George and they both headed for the exit.

George called the meeting back to order. One by one, Trevor announced the new Lyceum ambassadors. As they stepped forward they were greeted with applause and encouragement, especially the last to be announced, which was George Aguilera.

Once all the ambassadors had been given their charge, George adjourned the meeting.

As the meeting broke up, 'Bud' Vatave approached Dr. Glenn and said, "You're right on! I understand where you're coming from, and I have the program that will solve the problem."

Wincing inside, Dr. Glenn smiled and nodded politely. There was always someone who had "the solution."

Chapter 11

Making Inductive and Deductive Leaps

"Not everything that can be counted counts, and not everything that counts can be counted."
Albert Einstein

Seeking the Soul of Commerce

Chapter 11

The drive to Terra would have taken about 25 minutes at that time of day, a bit far to drive when it wasn't clear how long their conversation would last. So, Leonard suggested they sit on a bench in the park across the street from the Lodge where the Lyceum met.

On the way, while wondering where the conversation would lead, McKenzie said, "Does this count as our first official meeting?"

Leonard replied, "We agreed to talk and this is a good start."

They reached a bench, shaded by a large Cyprus and facing a memorial. Leonard gestured for McKenzie to sit first. "This looks safe enough, especially with that memorial cannon facing us."

Not quite in tune with Leonard's humor, McKenzie nodded once at the gesture, sat and said, "I appreciate the fact that we haven't had a chance to develop a relationship, but Terra contributes to the economy of this entire region, it affects everyone. The media has to cover it, and we can do a better job if you cooperate with us. It's not necessarily a one-way street.

"You need to know what's going on in the community, and to help us understand you better! You have to realize that now!"

Recalling Dr. Glenn's presentation, Leonard said, "Yes, I suppose, as 'stakeholders', we all do.

"So what do you want?"

"Leonard, we want more than a press release. I need to know how a leader thinks. I need to know what's going on in your mind as you're making decisions that affect not only your business but everyone in this community!"

"But, what goes on in my mind isn't 'news'." objected Leonard.

"I know. But it is part of what helps us understand how to approach the story, how to look for trends, what information to gather, how to serve our community. If we don't know anything about you, then we are constantly coming up short with what is going on in the company. All we have are numbers and statistics, and no way to attach meaning to them.

"For example, when I noticed how long it was taking you to find people to replace the senior executives who were leaving, I had no way of knowing what that signaled—if you were preparing to relocate to another community or country or what?"

"Where did that come from? We've been putting out notices, and you have the statistics, what else do you need?"

"But Leonard, I didn't have the statistics when I first noticed that they weren't being replaced."

Leonard nodded and said, "Fair enough. So where do we go from here? What do you want?"

"You wouldn't give me an interview."

"I wasn't avoiding you, McKenzie. Look, you of all people know that when I came to Terra, it was on the ropes. You were there! I had to focus on a whole series of internal issues, on aligning the organization with market expectations and trying to hang on to the remaining customers.

"For the first four years, I worked to transform Terra's culture, against internal resistance from those who thought the old ways of doing things were 'just fine'. The organization had gotten complacent, slid from market leadership, but wanted to hold on to heritage methods. It was on a fast track to extinction but refused to change."

"I heard things..."

"When I came on board, profits had shrunk to nothing, and they were facing layoffs. We had to invest in new ideas and technology, and rally people around them, but we had an aging workforce that—while quite capable at one time—had not been refreshed with enough new blood and had not kept up with new innovations. The old management team didn't see the changes coming in waste management, and refused to adapt when it was shown to them. They were stuck in trying to cope with daily crises they didn't understand. I had to let most of them go and bring in or move up a whole new management team."

"Like George."

Leonard replied, "Yes, he was the first person I moved up. But, with all that, talking to the press was just not on priority list. I had a business to run. So, if you tried to contact me, I expect Jane would shuttle you to Dennis, and he'd handle it."

McKenzie smiled and said, "Well, as Paul Harvey© would say, 'Now do I get to hear the rest of the story?'"

Leonard replied, "That will take more than the five minutes it takes for Paul Harvey© to tell his.

McKenzie nodded in assent and Leonard said, "One of my most interesting courses while working on my MBA was in organizational dynamics. It was based on the work of an Organizational Psychologist named McKinsey.[3] The basic concept is that you need to look at an organization as a system, and to ensure that all elements of the organization operate in alignment with each other. For instance, imagine if a car had all four tires pointed in different directions. It couldn't go anywhere.

"The same is true for an organization. It must have a common vision, understood by everyone in the organization, that is based on a common set of values. To implement a

---

[3] See Bibliography.

vision based on those values, you have to have a strategy, an organizational structure, a set of organizational systems, people with the right skill sets, management leading with the right style, and staffing actions, all fully aligned with the vision.

"But when I arrived, just getting the leadership to recognize that change was required, much less thinking that we needed to address every part of the business, was very hard.

"Some of the leadership team took to the concept quickly, some took a bit longer, and some fought the change. For some, the way they had always done their jobs was good enough. For me, it was vintage, not cutting edge, and I had to push them out."

McKenzie nodded and said, "I remember. That was, what, a couple months after you arrived. A number of managers left. Some of them said it was because you were impossible to get along with, but that was sour grapes?"

Leonard said, "It's tough on people when you hire them for one thing at a point in their lives when they think they have plenty of time to get really good at it. But getting good and efficient at doing a job can also make someone complacent. They often forget to look around and keep an eye on what's going on in the bigger market place like who's trying to eat their lunch. Our nation's largest auto manufacturer has let go of thousands of people lately. My sources tell me many people who lost their jobs simply never believed it would happen. Many had turned their backs on every opportunity to go back to school, to learn some new skills or even improve what they already knew. And then, things seem to change for them overnight, even when the signs have been around for years. Wouldn't the blame for a human catastrophe like that belong to the media as well as the company who let the people go?"

McKenzie replied, "George says most people don't want to change, most of the time, and won't until they're forced to."

"That's right," said Leonard, "but once we created a vision and had the right management team in place, we worked hard to get everyone in Terra pulling in the same direction. There were two key thrusts, first on quality and the other on customers.

"We used the term 'quality' as a rallying cry for everything... 'do it right the *first* time,' and developed metrics that allowed everyone in Terra to measure and see how they were doing."

"Everyone?"

"Yes. Everything we do in Terra has a process. At first there were disagreements about what the processes were, so we reviewed everything we did, literally using butcher paper on the walls to diagram every process we had."

"Sounds like a lot of work. How long did it take?"

"Seven months. More really; it never stops. Most people outside of a process-oriented business don't have any idea what it takes to map those processes. But we did it for everything, not only what my management team does to track costs, but what our employees do in their daily jobs.

"For instance, almost everyone in Chantilly has a lawn. Do you?"

"I own a condo."

"Which has a lawn in and around the units?"

McKenzie nodded yes and Leonard continued with, "Consider everything it takes to keep those lawns green. You have to water it, fertilize it, mow it, replant it, and kill bugs in it once in a while. But how many people, even on the same street, do any of that in the same way, on the same schedule, or get the same results?

"At Terra, and in almost any industry, we have to get the same results, each and every time, and on time. That's why we agreed to processes; processes that yield the same results each and every time, with predictable cost, time, and resource requirements, so that we can run a business and meet our customer needs."

"We could probably use a bit of this 'process management' at the Chronicle," McKenzie commented. "I can't tell you how many times we've run into problems because someone did something a little different without thinking about the impact it might have on other parts of the paper."

Leonard replied, "I've used this process in small and large businesses, in Boy Scouts and other volunteer groups. Anytime people work together, doing the same thing over and over again, even the simple process of writing down who does what when makes a big difference. You've also hit on the next key point in Terra's transformation.

"A business is about people working with people, both internal to the company and external, in the marketplace. As we mapped out our processes, we learned that there are many interface points where we find customers and suppliers.

"In most businesses, 'customers' are those they sell products or services to, and 'suppliers' are external sources of raw materials and supplies. Well, many of us had to learn that we had internal customers and suppliers as well. We concluded that everyone needed to think about customers the same way, whether internal or external to the business. So we created five key questions that everyone in Terra now has to answer about their customers.

"First they have to ask, 'Who are my customers?'

"With that defined, they then have to ask those customers, 'What are your expectations?'

"The effects of those two questions were amazing! Customers and suppliers began to understand each others needs and interests.

"The third question was, 'How do customers *measure* their expectations?' This enabled us to create a set of metrics that every team posts on the wall and many talk about every day, because it's what's *important to the customer* that matters. Not only did we put in place a whole new set of business measurements, we also found that we were spending money on things that no one cared about. So, we stopped spending the money, which was a huge increase in efficiencies and financial performance.

"The fourth question relates directly to the third as it was simply, 'How are we are doing against the expectations?'

"The final question is one that we use as the basis for generating improvements throughout the company, and that is, 'What are we doing to improve?'"

McKenzie contemplated this for a moment and asked, "So, when I was shuttled to your Communications Director, which role was I, customer or supplier? Were you fishing for information from me or trying to provide me with information? I could never tell if what I was saying was getting through at all, and you know I have a lot of files on Terra, and a huge amount on related business and community activities."

Leonard smiled and said, "McKenzie, the first time our Communications Director met with you, I didn't know anything about it. As I said, the Press just wasn't on my radar. Since then, well... Recently, largely because of you, we've put the Chronicle in our 'customer' category, because of the amount of print the Press has focused on Terra—particularly on the issue of our aging workforce."

McKenzie nodded and said, "So, who do I see now, you or your Communications Director?"

Leonard paused to assimilate what McKenzie appeared to be saying. He'd had painful dealings with reporters in large cities whose sole focus was on 'getting out the story', and it was a bit... refreshing... to find one who, like McKenzie, appeared to be genuinely interested in what he had to say. And he could see, now, that from her perspective, her stories hadn't been attacks on him and Terra, but statements of concern on behalf of the community. Given that, he decided to extend an olive branch and said, "It depends."

"On what?"

"On what it is you want. If you just want a 'story', then you and anyone else from the Press who wants that will be shuttled to our Communications Director. But, if your intent is to help Terra, then you'll talk with me. So, let me ask you, which is it going to be? What do you really want, McKenzie?"

McKenzie couldn't tell if she had won or lost a negotiation, but she knew she'd gained an opportunity to have a close working relationship with Chantilly's leading businessman. She paused to consider her words and said, "You don't really know much about me, do you?"

A big grin suddenly came across Leonard's face and he said, "Well, I know you've been pushed around a lot."

McKenzie looked puzzled, but decided to moved on. "Well, I suppose the best way to tell you 'what I really want' is to explain why I am so interested in Terra.

"I grew up here in Chantilly, middle and high schools, and came back about twenty years ago as the new journalism teacher at Chantilly High. Clay had been the Principal for about five years, and had put in place what some educators call 'portfolio management,' but Clay just called it a 'senior project.'

Chapter 11

"He felt it was important for graduating students to demonstrate that some part of what they had learned in school could be tied together and applied outside of school. A former small business owner, Clay used the Lyceum to help talk up the concept, and many of the local businesses started asking to see the projects as part of the job interview process.

"The Press got in the act and wrote articles about some of the students' work.

"One year, a group of my journalism students chose to do an investigative report on agricultural waste management as their senior project. Terra had just received a major grant from the National Science Foundation to investigate the viability of integrated agricultural waste management. Some of the students were farmers' kids. Everyone around here has some interest in farming, and like a lot of kids, they got really excited at the idea of helping to make the world better. So 'agricultural waste' was a reality to them.

"You weren't in agricultural waste before Terra, so I don't know if you know, but up to that point all agricultural waste products were handled separately and competed for limited space and resources. But the margins were so low and the capital costs so high that no one was doing well at really making this a business. However, with the potential payoff of a huge, unrecognized resource, there was an awful lot of interest across the agricultural community. So, a lot of people became interested in the project, including that handful of journalism students who selected it as the focus of their project.

"The students took great pains in doing their research, and I took great pride in watching them apply what they had learned in my class. After a few months, not only had they developed a good understanding of the technologies being used by the different waste management organizations, they also developed some thoughts on how Terra could improve on their efforts.

"One of the rules for the senior project allowed the students to interview people in the community, and a couple of the students developed some pretty strong ties with a couple of Terra's engineers. In the end, the project was one of the most successful ever. Two of the four students were offered intern positions at Terra during their summer breaks from college, and went on to become full time employees at graduation."

"What about their story?" asked Leonard.

"Well, that was a bit controversial. The NSF funding was a multi-year grant that showed real promise, but during the same period as the grant, Terra was deteriorating. The kids thought the company was attempting to grow too fast, chasing every opportunity they could find and not focusing enough on their core business. That's what they finally wrote, I agreed with them, and that's what we printed in the school paper.

Leonard grinned and said, "So that was your first story on Terra?"

"Yep, a student report, but it left me with a wealth of knowledge about and contacts at Terra, and a reputation as a local outside expert.

"The Chronicle heard about the story and wanted to follow up, and so their editor contacted me. I was saving money for the down payment on my condo, so I started doing a little freelance work, trying to uncover what was 'really' going on at Terra. That's how I met George, Trevor Brown, and your predecessor, Dan Blank.

"I left Chantilly High when they cut back the Journalism program, and transferred over to the grade school."

"That's how we met, wasn't it?" asked Leonard.

"Yes, I was leading a field trip to Terra. But those ended when they refocused on "core subjects" only.

Chapter 11

About then Anna Somers offered me a full time job at the Chronicle, and I took it."

"You seem to know a lot about the history of Terra," remarked Leonard. "What do you know about the current situation?"

"Well, your predecessor wasn't very talkative, and you haven't been either, up until now. So what I know is mostly from my own research. Basically, Terra seems to have done well financially under you, up to now. Your explanation of what you've been doing, the 'process management,' helped fill out things. But this new crisis, the problem with the aging workforce, seems to have snuck up on you. It looks like you're losing essential people—senior managers and engineers—to retirement, can't find replacements, and don't have any ready-made or simple solutions. Is that it?"

Leonard nodded once and said, "Well McKenzie, this has been very interesting. You've opened my eyes a bit. I guess we do share common interests, and good reason for continued discussion. But first, we need to get one thing straight.

"You know a lot more about things from a community perspective, but I know the business aspects and implications. It seems to me that it takes both perspectives, community and business, to understand this problem. You may want to help the community, but you need a story, and I need some new employees. So, I tell you what. I'll talk with you, if the stories you write are aimed at helping solve the workforce problem, rather than just getting headlines. OK?"

McKenzie frowned and said, "Leonard, I'm a journalist, a good one. If there's a story there, I'll find it, and I won't cover anything up or spin it for anyone. But this 'workforce' problem, what Dr. Glenn said, it worries me. I've seen how it's affecting you at Terra, and at other local businesses, and if something isn't done... Well, this is too big a problem for business or the Press. We need to work together, and I'm willing to give it a shot.

Leonard nodded and asked, "When should we meet again?"

Chapter 12

Media Reflects Culture
and
Culture is Reflected in the Media

"We've reached such an incredible level of freedom that, for the first time in history, we have to manage our own mutation. It's up to us to decide what it means to be a successful human being. That's the philosophical task of the age. ... The new economy just happens to be the form that our existential challenge takes today. As always the real obstacle is life itself."

Peter Koestenbaum

Seeking the Soul of Commerce

Chapter 12

The car door slammed shut with a solid thump, and McKenzie turned the key in the ignition. Traffic was relatively clear. The guards at the front gate were expecting her and had a pass ready, so when she steered her car into a visitor's slot, she was almost on time.

Leonard's assistant, Jane, looked up from her monitor, smiled in greeting and said, "McKenzie." Still smiling, she rolled out from behind her desk and stood, while saying, "His earlier meeting is running a bit late, and he asked me to show you right in." Jane ushered McKenzie into a small, private conference room and asked, "Is there anything you need? Coffee? Tea?" McKenzie said, "No, I'm fine," and Jane left; closing the door behind her.

The room was a small version of a corporate conference room, with the usual furnishings and presentation tools, but personal touches to the décor that gave it a 'homey' feel. As McKenzie took her notebook out of her briefcase and set it up in front of the head chair, she wondered if Jane or Mrs. Allegren was responsible for the personal touches. She'd finished, and was gazing out the window at the courtyard below, when the other door opened.

Leonard walked in from his private office and said, "McKenzie! Welcome. How have you been?"

"Busy, looking into our problem."

"'Our' problem?"

"I think it's bigger than we thought. Look at this..." McKenzie waved toward her notebook. Leonard sat in the chair facing it, at the head of the table. McKenzie sat on his right, picked up the notebook's remote, pointed at the screen and said, "All of my research shows that nearly everyone is finding it harder and harder to locate skilled employees. Not just technical, engineering types, but all kinds of skills. Take for instance Chantilly GM, where I have my Buick repaired." McKenzie pressed the remote, and a photo of the dealership appeared on the screen.

She pressed it again, and Leonard found himself looking at a balding, middle-aged man standing in front of a row of eight pneumatic car lifts. Behind him, a row of equally elderly men in overalls stood in front of the lifts, and she said, "This is the Maintenance Manager, Ricardo Alvarez. He told me that the average age of his mechanics is over 50, and he can't find new apprentices. He's put offers out at $20 an hour, nearly $42K a year plus benefits for high school graduates, and can't get any takers. He says the schools aren't training kids in auto mechanics any more, that he's complained numerous times, but that they haven't done anything about it.

"I tried to contact the Director of the Occupational Programs at the Chantilly School District, but there isn't one."

"Director or program?"

"Well... both. The District has four high schools and seven middle schools. Back in 1980, between them, those eleven schools had 71 trade and technical teachers. Now, the middle schools have none, zero. The high schools have twelve, and all of those are well over fifty. Only Chantilly High still has a shop program worth mentioning. It's being kept alive by direct grants by your C.R. department, and even it will probably disappear over the next eight years as the teachers retire."

"What? What happened?"

"This is Ralph Floyd, the last Director of the District's Occupational Program. This is Ralph giving certificates to graduates of the mechanics program. Here he's awarding woodshop program grads, here to metal shop, electrical, HVAC, and plastics. Ralph retired in '89, and they never replaced him.

"I also talked with Janet Reams, the Curriculum Director for Chantilly Unified, checked our files at the Chronicle, and researched the national situation. As near as I can tell, shop and technical courses have been withering away everywhere, due to four root causes.

"First, there's the growing emphasis on basic academics that started in the '80s. Remember the argument over numbers between Edra and Houston?"

Leonard nodded and McKenzie said, "The District's achievement is measured by, and their state funding depends on, how well their enrolled students do on the state tests, and those tests only measure academic subjects. So, Chantilly Unified, like most districts nationally, has been moving funding from trade and technical programs to basic academics.

"As options other than academics have gone down, and pressure to perform academically has gone up, the students who do not perform well academically have dropped out in increasing numbers—Just as Dr. Glenn pointed out. This drains off the 'lowest performing' students and increases the apparent performance of schools in the state tests."

Leonard nodded and said, "Which is why Edra interprets the numbers the way she does."

"Yep. She *has* to look at the academic performance of current students."

Leonard said, "But it's a false measurement."

"From Houston's perspective, but not from Edra's."

McKenzie pressed the remote again. A picture of the Chelsea University administration building appeared and she said, "The next main factor is the vastly increased emphasis, overemphasis really, on college and college prep courses. There are a number of commonly accepted reasons for this, but they're not the whole story.

"The first reason, of course, is that high school grads are no longer ready to join the workforce. Even if they can read and write, they don't have marketable skills because the skills programs have been removed from the high school curricula even as the demand for technical skills has increased.

"Another is the increase in lifelong earnings, $900,000 more—in 1999 dollars—for a four year degree, as compared to high school graduates. However, that's *current*, relatively unskilled, high school graduates. I've tried to find earnings comparisons between college grads and technically skilled high school grads, but I couldn't find any.

"None?"

"None."

Leonard said, "So the income comparison between high school and college grads is a false comparison of artificially unskilled high school grads with skilled college grads."

"Yes. And yet another, difficult to assess, reason for the emphasis is the importance our society places on college education as an indication of success. People who have college degrees are assumed to be more successful as people, and their parents are assumed to be more successful as parents, than are those without college degrees. In addition, a high school's academic program is often measured by the percentage of their students who go on to college.

"However, all of this shortchanges the vast majority of students. The 2000 Census indicates that 24 percent of high school graduates, aged 25 or older, obtained a bachelors degree. So, despite all the emphasis on academics and moving on to college, only about a fourth of high school grads go on to complete a four year degree.

Chapter 12

Leonard nodded in agreement and said, "Half of my employees have college degrees, and the other half don't."

McKenzie continued with, "Yes. The myth that 'success is defined by college' is very powerful, and it can be crippling. It fails to recognize, like you just said, that fully half the jobs do not require a college education, but do require education beyond high school. And most jobs require life-long learning and retraining.

"Because the high school shop and other skills programs were undervalued, they were cancelled in favor of college prep programs, when in fact 75% of the kids needed them. An unintended consequence is a shrinking pool of trade and technical instructors, making it very difficult to bring those programs back. Unlike most academic teachers, shop teachers can make a lot more practicing their trade than teaching it, and none of the four-year schools in this state, not even the state universities, have programs to produce trade or technical teachers. As a result, we just aren't producing new shop teachers. In fact, a high percentage of our remaining shop teachers are former mechanics, machinists, or builders who got a teaching certificate and went into teaching *after* retiring from their trade. The others are all well into their fifties, and the district is not hiring new instructors as they retire.

"Now, a few scattered schools are bringing back shop and technical classes, but often as a preparation for advanced technical training or college degree programs. They're not actually preparing kids to enter the workforce, and the graduates of the programs aren't... well... let me tell you about Tim, the younger nephew of a girlfriend of mine. Tim is in his early twenties, is engaged to a very nice girl, and works in the building trades with his dad.

"His dad didn't do that well academically—not bad,

just not well—but he did very well in shop classes. Metal shop, wood shop, drafting, auto mechanics, welding, he loved it all. Over the years he's been a CNC machinist, a truck driver, a welder, and now he drives large earth moving equipment.

"Now his son Tim also did poorly academically, but there was no shop program at his middle school, and none worth mentioning at his high school, so he dropped out at sixteen and went to work with his dad—as soon as he got his driver's license. I understand he's a pretty good driver now. The problem is, that's all he knows and all he can do. Last spring he brought home a puppy— he's always been good with animals. His family kept reminding him to build a doghouse for it, but he never did, until the weather changed and he had to. Then he scrounged some lumber, took it to his parent's place, and tried to put it together using his dad's tools. But he couldn't do it. There he was, 22 years old, a bright kid working in construction, and he couldn't build a doghouse. He'd never taken woodshop, he didn't take drafting, he didn't know how to design and build something. All he knew was how to drive big earth moving equipment."

Leonard frowned, gazed directly at McKenzie, paused and then said, "I think it's bigger than that."

"What's bigger?" asked McKenzie

"The way you're describing the issue. It's not that he was a dummy or unsuccessful. He was driving a big piece of equipment and probably making $30.00 an hour. It's that he didn't know how to relate his success in one activity to another activity."

McKenzie jumped in and said, "So what you're saying is, he didn't know how to transfer what he knew to other areas. Youngsters growing up are not coming away with creative, critical thinking. Tim was not practiced in taking what he learned in one area and apply-

ing it in another area.

"So, in some ways, Tim seems to be fairly typical of current kids. He didn't learn how to think creatively, to turn what he knew into something of value in the marketplace. But there are some important differences too, and that gets me to the fourth root cause of the loss of skills, the attitudes of the kids.

"In the absence of anything meaningful or important to do or to belong to, kids look for something, anything, to give them a sense of belonging, of identity, of importance. For a lot of kids that means being 'cool'. If you're 'cool', then other kids accept you, look up to you, seek you out, and try to be like you. And of course, in order to be 'cool' you have to avoid things that are not cool, which at this point apparently includes most of the trades and technical occupations. So, the kids who can, choose college—which *is* 'cool'—and those who don't see college as an option, don't see much left to choose from and seem to just bounce around for a while."

Leonard crinkled his brows and asked, "When did that happen? When I was in school, all the 'cool' guys were in the shop classes."

McKenzie replied, "Well Leonard, the shop classes are all gone.

Leonard said, "So where'd they go, and how do the kids practice what they learn?"

McKenzie replied, "At the mall, when they choose between one brand of tennis shoes and another.

"The real question is how and why that happened? What changed the kid's attitudes? Why are schools pushing everyone toward college? Why the drop in technical education at all levels, including college?

"We've already looked at catastrophic social changes, the loss of roots, relationships, and purpose that kids had before World War II and the urbanization and media impact Dr. Glenn talked about. Remember, when you were born on a farm, you mattered, you were part of a family who depended on your contribution to survive.

"I've discussed this with George, and he agrees. We also looked at what our culture as a whole, our media in particular, has substituted for the old communal sense of purpose and place, and how they're doing it."

Leonard said, "That sounds reasonable. You're the media expert. What did you come up with?"

McKenzie took a deep breath, let it out with a sigh and said, "Well, first, let's make sure we have a common frame of reference."

"Like with the word 'communication'," Leonard replied, referring to the conversation that led to the visit.

McKenzie smiled and nodded and said, "'Media' covers a broad range of methods of transmitting information. Those methods or media include TV, magazines, books, radio, the internet, CDs and DVD's, newspapers, and iPods ®. But as different as they are, they have one thing in common. They're all tools for delivering information, information that has been carefully shaped and crafted for their exact format."

Leonard frowned and said, "I understand the notion that most messages are carefully crafted and shaped. After all, my communications department works to get out the 'right' message all the time. But aren't some messages, like news and education, supposed to be shared without adding bias or spin to the information?"

"But everyone has a bias, Leonard. The people producing the news, writing the textbooks, always have a point of view. One of the first things a reporter decides when beginning a story is the point of view they'll take, or the 'angle.'"

Chapter 12

"Angle?"

"The twist or perspective that will make the story most interesting for the readers."

"Oh? Every story?"

"Yes. The angle is what determines the direction of your research and how you tell the story. For instance, in a 'dog saves boy' story, the angle is how special the dog is for saving the boy, so you focus on the dog, not the boy."

"So, what's the 'angle' here? What makes Terra so special you keep coming back?

"The *local* angle. The people of Chantilly aren't interested in a huge, national, workforce problem. But they are deeply interested in local jobs. So, what makes Terra so special is that it was where I discovered the problem, and it's what keeps the people of Chantilly interested in the problem."

"So you're using Terra to make a point?"

"Look, my, our, research shows that the problems you're having aren't unique to Terra. In fact, my next feature story is aimed at the national market and shows how business and industry across the country are experiencing the same problems you're having here."

"Why go national?"

"Well, my editor thinks there might be a Pulitzer in it, but that's secondary. I became a reporter in the first place to help Chantilly. That's still my main goal, but this is a national problem and has to be solved nationally."

Leonard nodded and said, "So, what are you going to say?"

"In the first article I'll stick to the basics—the aging workforce and inadequate number of skilled youngsters moving into the marketplace."

"Think anyone will listen?"

"Not yet. The high tech industry hasn't quite realized that their investments in education are futile, because the present education system *can't* deliver what they need. Oh, they'll try to get education to change, and the educators will point at their 'successes' like incorporating computers into the classroom, and, as a result, making parents and students believe that by just using a computer kids can now move into the computer industry and have marketable skills for success. When the fact is the true value of computers has not been realized. Instead, they've just been brought into the classroom like a pad of paper or a calculator. We're beginning to see that there's far more potential. But for most, it just remains a tool.

"And then there's the high-tech game, music, and video devices. Many of the kids spend more time on those than they do in class, and it's mostly time spent sitting passively rather than moving around and interacting with each other.

"Even industry and venture capitalists thought there would be this great market that wasn't."

"The 'dotbomb'."

"Yep. It was fed by fantasies of 'quick riches' and the 'good life,' and hyped by the media until being a rich geek became totally 'cool'. But did you buy in?"

"Terra? No. Some of our financial managers suggested we invest, but none of the start-ups they pitched could predict when they'd go liquid."

"Huh?"

"Oh, sorry. They didn't know when, how, or if they'd ever earn money. However, Terra, and many others, began to see how to incorporate computers as an integral part of their business process—in combination with knowledge and tools—that enabled us to do many things we hadn't been able to do before."

McKenzie said, "Prior to the dotbomb, I read about a few nay-saying financial managers. People said they

164

Chapter 12

'just didn't *get* it' and ostracized them for being uncool.

"And that's part of the point. Look at what happened there. Kids flocked to a particular set of technical occupations because they were 'cool'. It had nothing to do with reality. Many of them could have made as much or more, with less effort and risk, in other technical occupations."

Leonard said, "But those weren't cool."

McKenzie replied, "Right. So, let's look at what influences the attitudes and behaviors of those who will, we hope, replace the current workforce. Why do they make the choices they do? I think you'll be very surprised at how differently they respond to messages, to demands for their time and attention, than your current workforce. Probably the best way to explain it is to play a DVD I've brought. Do you have some time?

"Leonard glanced at his watch and said, "Yes."

<hr>

For nearly an hour, Leonard watched in amazement and disbelief as a Public Broadcasting Service program called "The Merchants of Cool" played on the screen. When the credits began to scroll, McKenzie turned it off and asked, "Now do you see what we're up against?"

"It's a feedback loop. Those... 'cool hunter' teams spy on kids, find 'trend setters' and 'early adopters', and produce and feed it back to the kids."

McKenzie nodded and replied, "Often under the kids' radar, so the kids don't realize they're being sold something, something that was theirs to begin with."

"How big did they say the market was?"

"$150 billion."

Leonard said, "We always tried to spend time with Bruce, but I... well, it takes a lot of work to run a big company. I missed a lot of evenings and weekends, and then he started wanting *things* instead of us. And so we spend our time away from home so we can buy things for our families, because we don't have time to be with them."

"Another loop," said McKenzie

Leonard nodded and replied, "And most of it's dominated by the big-five media giants. I suppose they have to, but their approach..."

McKenzie said, "They convince the kids to buy what they're selling: clothing, music, movies, television, food, whatever, by packaging it in 'cool'. They aren't accountable for these kids, who they are, their future, their emotional or physical health, or the real value or effect of their products."

"You have to give us that; Terra's products actually help people. We fill a real need."

McKenzie shook her head and replied, "It's not about helping or filling a need. It's that someone else is accountable for the kids, *not* media or industry. They're not accountable!"

Leonard grimaced and said, "By appealing to the lowest common denominator; portraying boys as crude, rude, loud, and obnoxious."

"And girls as sex-flaunting nymphets whose main asset is their body."

Leonard said, "All that about the downward spiral of sex and violence, carrying on during 'spring break' like they were on the set of some MTV® show.

McKenzie nodded and said, "They haven't seen, experienced any real 'life', all they know is what they've seen on screens."

"It's that giant feedback loop again. The media sells an image of kids to kids, the kids imitate that, and the media records it and feeds it back to them."

"And if the kids turn and fight, the battle itself is recorded, packaged, and fed right back to them."

Chapter 12

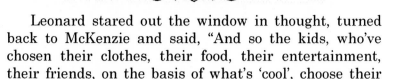

Leonard stared out the window in thought, turned back to McKenzie and said, "And so the kids, who've chosen their clothes, their food, their entertainment, their friends, on the basis of what's 'cool', choose their careers the same way?"

"It's one of the factors, yes, but a big one."

"McKenzie, I'm not comfortable with this. I deal with hard facts, logical business demands, guided by a benevolent set of principles. This is... it's not what I'm used to, and I don't like it. I don't like it a lot!"

"I'm sorry Leonard. I didn't mean to make you uncomfortable."

"I know..."

Leonard stared in thought some more, then asked, "Did they just say that education doesn't happen just in school, but everywhere?"

"Basically, yes. They learn as much or more about the world from the media as they do from school and family, not only how to dress and what to eat, but how to make decisions about relationships, from stories and messages shot at them by TV, the net, billboards, magazines, music, movies, video games. It's not new, it's been going on since before Elvis."

"I can handle Elvis. At least he had some real life experiences and challenges that shaped his ideas about how to perform and what was important. *The Merchants of Cool*© makes it clear that advertisers want people to believe they don't need to have real experiences to get respect and self-esteem. That all that kids need to do is make the right buying choices. Education programs that want them to think about things, or build things, or learn how to think for themselves, are 'too tough', and 'not cool'. We can't fix a problem that is so much bigger than schools. The problem is so big, any single solution is overwhelmed. How can we possibly reach young people, get them thinking about their future, if all they think about is the next 'cool' thing they want to do, or the next 'cool' thing the marketers want them to buy or do?"

McKenzie smiled and said, "I asked George that after he showed me '*Merchants*'."

Intrigued, Leonard lifted his left brow and said, "George? What'd he say?"

"He said, 'It's simple, McKenzie. They're selling illusions, you offer real life.'"

"What does that mean?" asked McKenzie.

"I think it means we start offering people what they *really need*, the education, work experience, opportunities to build relationships that are best for *them*," Leonard replied.

"Heh. Have you ever tried to get a child to do something because it was 'good for them?'" asked Leonard.

"I was a teacher, remember," replied McKenzie."

"OK, so how do we do it here?" Leonard asked.

"I don't know, but with your help, I think we can put a team together and begin finding out. Right here in Chantilly," McKenzie said.

"Like who?" asked Leonard.

"Well... George, of course, and Trevor, Houston, Dr McPhearson, Dr Gedissman, and Buck Olsen. They represent difference stakeholders of the community, and should be part of this," said McKenzie.

"Stakeholders?" Leonard sat back in his chair, blinked a few times and said, "Ah, yes. I guess I am one now, but I'm really struggling with this... An hour ago I was trying to get my own team aligned with the problem, and now you want to bring in people who know next to nothing about my business, are all over the map with their opinions, and you think they'll get something done? Come on!"

"OK, it seems a bit far fetched, but hasn't anyone

explained to you what a stakeholder is? You were at the Lyceum; this is not about you and your business anymore. The whole point of the video is that everyone is looking in the wrong direction. This issue is bigger than schools, it's bigger than Terra, and you can't change it by yourself no matter how many outreach programs you fund. The old way of everyone having their own program isn't working. You *know* that now! So it's time to do something different. It's time to call on higher principles, like we use at the Lyceum, like those that created this country. Leonard, I know this isn't easy, but you're a respected leader, and this community will listen to you."

Leonard paused in thought for a full minute, then said, "Leave the DVD. I have to talk to some of my key people. If I can convince them, I'll give you a call."

McKenzie ejected *The Merchants of Cool©* from her notebook, and handed it to Leonard. He saw her out, and as she left, she overheard Leonard say, "Jane, schedule a meeting of the management team. There's something they need to see.

Chapter 13

Shaping the Problem, Building the Team, and Aligning the People

"Life seeks to organize so that more life can flourish... Life wants to happen. Life is unstoppable."
Margaret Wheatley, and Myron Kellner-Rogers

Chapter 13

Leonard turned off the DVD, turned up the lights, and scanned the faces of his crisis team. Amanda Caldwell looked surprised and bewildered, like she didn't see the connection between *The Merchants of Cool*® and her job as H.R. Director. Marci Baker, the C. & E.R. Manager, was nodding her head, Dennis Aiken, the Communications Director, was smiling in admiration, and Rusty Hawkins, the Director of Waste Management Engineering, looked like he was waiting for more information.

After assessing their expressions, Leonard turned to Amanda and asked, "Amanda, what do you think?"

Amanda blinked and replied, "Well, I'm not sure. I mean, it changes how I view a lot of things... You know, I sometimes brag to my neighbor, Susie, that my son is the district manager of a major sports shoe company. He says they make the 'coolest' shoes on the market. He always wears the latest designer labels, has the latest CDs, and owns a car most kids his age would die for. But, he buys a new pair of shoes, or something else, before he pays his bills, and then begs me to rescue him. Happens all the time, and he always promises to cut back the spending, to 'be responsible'. But after a month or two, he's back to the same old habits. I guess I thought I was a bad parent for not teaching him how to manage money.

"After seeing this, well, it's a relief to know that maybe it's not me, or not just me. But it's kind of frightening too. It makes me feel, well, helpless and angry. As his mother I should have been able to... but, Harold and I both have to work just to get by, and it's frightening to see our children growing up believing they deserve a lot for very little effort."

Leonard nodded and said, "As a parent myself, I can

appreciate that. My son shows the same symptoms, and I can't tell you how angry it makes me. And I suppose I have to look at my own behavior as closely as I do his. But do you see how those symptoms are affecting our business, our workforce problem?"

"Well... It does explain a lot about young, inexperienced applicants. Kids looking for a job have a lot of unrealistic expectations about pay and quick advancement in the organization, and their work ethic is nonexistent. They never ask what they can do for Terra or describe what they have to contribute; instead it's 'I want to be a senior manager'. It's all about what the company can do for them."

"The other day while interviewing a young woman I asked her if she had any particular skills that she thought it would be helpful for me to know about. And she said, 'Well, my 'parallel thinking streams' are pretty advanced.'

"Of course, I asked what that was and she said, 'I can have a many as 11 windows opened on my screen at once, talking with 5 people, browsing with 2 servers, checking out the news, watching a video clip, playing music, you know?"

"What impresses me most about that sort of thing is the fact that they think multitasking while sitting in front of a computer screen is impressive. But it reminds me of my mom. When I was growing up she routinely kept twice that many streams of thought and activity going in real time—what with 5 kids and a husband needing dinner, clothes, food bought, prepared and on the table on time, car gassed and ready for delivery to theater practice, ball games, and PTA meetings, all with the wash done, a pot of soup for our neighbor and still getting the dog walked before my dad came home.

"And I was supposed to be impressed by someone sitting

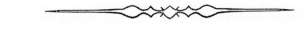

on their behind in front of a computer screen? Come on!

"I'm still holding out for people with what George called real 'touchy-feely' experience."

Leonard thanked Amanda, turned to Marci and asked, "So, Marci, what did you think?"

Marci replied, "I'm not really sure. My kids are still too young to know what a designer label is."

Leonard asked, "They're what, three and one?"

Marci smiled and replied, "Yes. It seems like something I should know about, but I don't know what I could do about it as a parent. I mean, like they said, the media is everywhere. We can't lock our children away."

Leonard said, "No, we can't, but maybe we can figure out what we *can* do. What do you think as the Director of Community Relations?

"Well, last week we received a grant request from a program on media literacy. My guys haven't processed it yet because it's the first time I've heard of it, and we're still looking into it. It seems like there should be some connection, but I need time to examine their program. Is there anything specific you'd like me to do?"

Leonard replied, "Yes there is, but we'll get to that in a moment."

Then he turned to his Communications Director and asked, "Dennis?"

Dennis started and said, "Me? Well, they have a much more impressionable market than we do, with our hard-assed customers. The kids are a lot more, what, changeable. Our customers have a lot more experience, pretty reliable needs and expectations, and once we sell them, they stay sold, as long as we keep delivering good product. It's a lot easier for us to get repeat business. Besides, what we're doing benefits everyone. So we don't really need to manipulate people, just do a good job describing the benefits."

Leonard asked, "How does what the media is doing affect us?"

Dennis ran his tongue over his upper incisors and said, "Well, the kids Amanda sends me, their attitudes are like she said, and they don't seem to have any idea how to talk with people. It's like they're 'conversation challenged' or something. I'm having a very difficult time finding new hires who can really interact with our employees, suppliers, customers, or the media, and I suppose this helps explain why."

Leonard looked at Rusty and raised a brow.

Rusty nodded and said, "Well... I'm not sure what any of this has to do with waste management."

Leonard smiled and asked, "Is it 'cool'?

"Waste management? What does that have to do with it?"

"You've heard Amanda and Marci talk about their recruitment problems. What's the main difficulty in your department?"

"With the applicants? Well, most of them have never built anything. A lot of my crew is about my age, or nearly, and when we were youngsters we built crystal radios, soap-box racers, tree houses, and made stuff with our chemistry sets. Later we bought old cars and turned them into hotrods. Most of these kids have never really built anything. They may say they've 'built' computers, but they didn't make the board and solder resisters and chips onto it, they just assembled parts. But just about all of us created stuff, just ask Dennis."

Dennis said, "Me! My chemistry set caught fire. I preferred the microscope set; I loved watching things wiggle in the swamp water. But yeah, most boys did that kind of thing. My brother and I had a tree house too."

Leonard grinned at his own fond memories, turned back to Rusty and asked, "So, kids today don't build

things like we used to. Why do you suppose that is?" Before he could respond, Leonard asked, "Remember the first skateboards?"

Rusty nodded and said, "Yeah, roller-skates nailed to the bottom of plywood boards. Oh, right, now corporations manufacture them, with 'cool' logos and endorsements. That's what happens every time kids start building something, isn't it? The corporations grab it, spruce it up, and sell them a 'cool' version. I guess, well, 'cool' gets in the way of 'creative'."

Leonard nodded, thanked Rusty, looked the four of them over and said, "I want you to go over your notes and continue thinking about the message in this video. As far as I can tell, the problem it describes is definitely part of our workforce problem, and our problem is just a small example of a looming national problem."

"National?" said Marci.

"Yes. Picture the problems we're having, but everywhere. It's not just us, our community, or our industry. It's *all* technical, skilled, and creative occupations. Now, of course there's no way we can do anything about that ourselves. Nothing we've done has, and I don't think anything we can do on our own will.

"Given that, since we can't solve the problem on our own—and make no mistake about this, it has to be solved or Terra won't survive—I think we have to expand our efforts by joining with a larger group of people, people from the community who are just as invested in solving the problem as we are, but have different perspectives, experience, talents. If we all work together on this, then maybe we can find some method or system of solving it.

"Now, Marci, I want you to put together a list of all the education related outreach programs that we fund locally. We need to know how much we spend, how long each program has been around, who it's supposed to help, how success is measured, if they're actually making a difference in some way, what a return on investment looks like when we compare programs, how many Terra volunteers participate in each program, and in what way the program relates to the economic development needs of the community."

Marci nodded and said, "We'll pull that together."

Leonard said, "Thanks Marci," then turned to Amanda..

"Now, Amanda. We've been wrestling for some time with the difficulties in finding people with the qualities and qualifications we need, now and moving forward. You've sifted through what, 210,000 resumes in order to replace 1,000 people in the past year. And even with all that, we haven't been able to fill our openings because of the limited skills of the applicants.

"Guys, that's 210 applicants for every opening. We don't have a labor shortage, we have a *skills* shortage.

"Dennis and Rusty, get together with Amanda's team, go over the skills deficits in your applicants, and compile a complete comparison between our current employees and our applicants. I want to know what the applicants are missing, where they're weak, and where they need improvement.

"Now, you all know I've been looking into this. I've learned some things in the last few weeks that have had a dramatic impact on my thinking. Last month, Dr. Stephen Glenn gave a presentation at the Lyceum on why today's kids aren't getting what they need to become capable, well-rounded people. What he said made a lot of sense and really helped clarify things for me. Jane managed to get copies of one of his CDs, and had it transcribed. On your way out, stop by her desk and pick them up. I want you and your teams to study them before you compile your reports.

Chapter 13

"Dr. Glenn raised some points that I hadn't really thought about before. As a business leader, I've always known the need to have people who can think well and work with others, but it was all in the context of getting a specific job done. It was about bringing their technical knowledge to solving problems. What Dr. Glenn talked about was something far more fundamental. And that is that we can't have people capable of solving problems unless they have the fundamental capabilities necessary to be successful at life in today's world... economic self sufficiency, the ability and desire to participate in our self governance, the ability to communicate and work with others, the ability to learn, unlearn, and relearn as technology and information advance, and the capability to prepare for the future. These are all skills we need at Terra, whether the employee works in Finance, H.R., Production, or Engineering. So study his presentation, and, when you consider your conclusions and recommendations, keep in mind that at some point you're going to have to share your conclusions with a larger group that includes people from the community. Yes, Dennis?"

"Will you be in charge of the new group?"

"Me? No, they'd think I was too business centered, and they'd probably be right. No, we'll need someone that everyone knows and trusts.

"Oh, by the way, Rusty, I need you to think about this too. I need you to build a systems model, but not like one you've built before. I need you to think about— and you'll need to work with Donna, Amanda, and Marci—on what a child's life cycle looks like."

Rusty gazed quizzically at Leonard and asked, "What do you mean 'a child's life cycle'? Isn't that what parents and educators are supposed to think about?"

Leonard replied, "Rusty, I think you're right, but, life has gotten really complex, and we all need to work

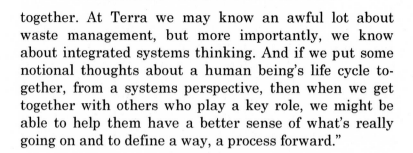
together. At Terra we may know an awful lot about waste management, but more importantly, we know about integrated systems thinking. And if we put some notional thoughts about a human being's life cycle together, from a systems perspective, then when we get together with others who play a key role, we might be able to help them have a better sense of what's really going on and to define a way, a process forward."

Jane had a cup of George's favorite brew ready for him—bitter-sweet chocolate in foamy milk, sweetened with a South American plant called stevia—and Leonard accepted a cup as well. They both smiled at the familiar ritual, sharing fond memories. Finally George broke the silence, by asking, "Alice and Bruce?"

Leonard replied, "Alice is fine, but Bruce is a lot of work. We're still exploring options. You and Donna? I've heard Mega Pixels is in trouble."

"We're worried about her retirement."

"They underfunded?"

"Apparently."

"I'm sorry to hear that. I hope things turn out, but if they don't, well, we still need you."

George said, "I was wondering how long it would be before you called."

Leonard cocked his head slightly, looked directly into George's eyes and said, "It's gotten worse since you left."

"Can't find a replacement?"

"Amanda says we'll probably have to break your old job into three positions. Nobody else can do everything you did, but that's not why I asked you to come in."

"Didn't think it was."

"I've had to take a very long, hard, look at the workforce problem, as you know, and I've come to several conclusions."

"Oh?"

"It's not just a business problem, it's everyone's problem. It's not just or even primarily an education problem. It's a problem with the entire community, and the only way we'll solve it will be by working together as a community.

"And how do you propose doing that?"

"McKenzie suggested putting together a group consisting of some of my managers and representatives from the community, such as Trevor, Houston, Dr. McPhearson, Dr. Gedissman, Buck Olsen, and you."

"That's an interesting group."

"Yes. Of course, someone would need to run herd on them, and it couldn't be me, too partisan. So, I was hoping you'd do it."

George blew gently on his brew and said, "You want me to use systems management to work toward a total community solution?"

"That's about it, yes. Will you do it?"

George hefted his cup and replied, "Let me finish this first."

McKenzie's shoes clicked across the gloomy KBCT TV parking lot to the 'staff' slot where she'd left her car. Once inside, she called her friend and mentor, Anna Somers, the Editor of the Chronicle.

"Anna," she said, "The station is being bought out by Winston-Kellogg. What have you heard?"

There was a long pause and then Anna said, "McKenzie, they usually go for cost savings by cutting local personnel, and increase advertising revenue by bringing in additional staff there. When does your contract run out?"

Chapter 14

Aligning Concepts
Around a Plan to Move Forward

"A Country, its people and leaders alike, has to be honest with itself and look clearly at exactly where it stands in relation to other countries and in relation to the flatteners. It has to ask itself, 'to what extent is my country advancing or being left behind by the flattening of the world, and to what extent is it adapting to and taking advantage of all the new platforms for collaboration and competition?' ... With China and the other nine flatteners coming on so strong, no country today can afford to be anything less than brutally honest with itself."

Thomas L. Friedman, *The World is Flat*, pp. 312 – 313

Jane said, "George." stood, gave him a long hug and asked, "How are you?"

"Unaccustomed to keeping a schedule. Have they been waiting?"

"McKenzie just got here. They're in Leonard's office. Your usual is on the table."

"Thanks"

Leonard and McKenzie greeted George as he entered. When everyone was seated around Leonard's table, George said, "I think we all know why we're here, but why don't the two of you bring me up to date on where you are. Leonard?"

Leonard nodded and said, "Let me start by thanking you for coming and helping us with this workforce issue sooner rather than later.

George nodded in acknowledgement and Leonard said, "Now, for the ten years I've been here, and for about forty years before that, Terra has been the most successful business in Chantilly. We've employed tens of thousands of local people over the years, always worked closely with the community leaders, and tried to be a good corporate citizen. Then..."

Leonard paused in thought for a moment and then said, "By God, George, you arranged Dr. Glenn's presentation on purpose, didn't you?"

George grinned and replied, "And the video. I've wanted to get you, McKenzie, and some of the others, into a room with Dr. Glenn for some time. When you joined the Lyceum, and I became President of our chapter, that gave me the opportunity to share with you some work that transformed my perspective on kids and our future."

With a wry smile, Leonard said, "Well, it worked.

His presentation, and *The Merchants of Cool©* video, sure made me realize how far my head was buried in the sand. I hadn't thought about how much influence the world outside our families and classrooms has on our children. Those of us in the business community need to have a higher visibility in the eyes of these kids."

"How so?" asked George.

"It's hard to describe. Terra still needs to be, and wants to be seen as, a good, strong, corporate citizen. But we're not as centralized in and around Chantilly as we were in the old days. We now have customers, suppliers, business partners and satellite facilities outside the state and in other countries. I had Jane do a quick review of my calendar for last week, and well over half my time is spent with business relationships, large and small, outside of the local area. The same is true for most of my managers and many of our employees.

"As Terra's focus expanded beyond Chantilly, more and more of our local community involvement's been grass roots activities by employees with solid interests here in Chantilly, and there've been less and less official corporate activities."

Leonard turned to McKenzie and said, "Like when we used to have school kids tour the place."

Turning back to George, he said, "But our corporate giving's still based on what we did in the past, rather than on what we need to do for the future. We just kept doing the same thing we'd always done.

"I can think of two reasons why we just kept doing the same old thing. The first is that the community kept treating us the same old way. They came around, asked for money, and assured us that, whatever else happened, they wouldn't ask us for much of our time. The second reason is that we established giving policies years ago, put people in place to administer that, and then didn't pay much attention. It's certainly not an area I knew or thought much about, and as long as we didn't look bad for not helping, that was all we knew to do."

Leonard blinked, recalled an old question and asked McKenzie, "Why *did* you leave teaching?"

McKenzie smiled and said, "The long version or the short version?"

Leonard replied, "Whichever."

"The short version, I simply disagreed with the way things were being run in the school, and with the overall philosophy of what it meant to educate the kids. Sometime we'll go into a longer explanation."

George sipped from his brew and said, "It sounds like you're getting a broader picture, and you've picked up some new terms along with the ideas. I think you'll find it much easier to talk with some of the others. Houston, E.T. Stroud, Trevor... You're beginning to form a common idea base and a broader terminology, but how would you describe the root problem?"

Leonard's brow crinkled above his nose, and he replied, "It's complex...with so many perspectives, issues, misconceptions, preconceptions, and expectations that most people would probably say it's not solvable. That said, from a business perspective, it seems to center around the need for alignment, assignment of accountability, and putting resources in place to solve the problem."

George turned to a grinning McKenzie and asked, "You approve?"

McKenzie hid her grin behind her cup as she sipped her coffee. Then she lowered the cup and replied, "We still need to formulate a clear statement of the problem, and to agree on an approach to a solution."

"Leonard nodded and said, "Bringing more people on board before we have a clear agreement would just create confusion—'Too many cooks.'"

George stood, said, "I have an idea," walked to a wall, and opened a door exposing a giant whiteboard. Then he picked up a black dry-erase pen, and drew a line down the middle of the board.

George turned so his left side was toward Leonard and McKenzie, pointed at the left side of the board with the pen and asked, "OK, what are the main areas of difficulty?"

Leonard said, "Workforce development" just as McKenzie said, "Education."

George grinned and wrote, "Education" in the upper left corner of the board, and "Workforce Dev." in the upper middle.

"OK, what are other aspects of this problem?"

Leonard nodded to McKenzie. She said, "Communications, family..." and Leonard said, "Business and government."

George wrote those in random spots on the left side of the board and said, "And?"

McKenzie waved to Leonard, who said, "Well...health and finance."

George wrote those down, while McKenzie stared at the board in thought. Then her face brightened and she said, "Media, politics, and... well... the whole 'vision' thing."

George said, "Very good, McKenzie."

"Leonard, anything else?"

Leonard shrugged and suggested, "If we're including 'vision,' then we should include 'process management'."

George said, "OK, that's probably enough and wrote, 'media,' 'politics,' 'vision,' and 'process mgt.' in scattered spots on the left half of the board. Then he stood back, gestured toward the board with his left hand and asked, "What do you notice about these categories?"

Leonard said, "Well, they're disorganized."

George nodded and said, "Anything else?"

Chapter 14

McKenzie replied, "They're not connected."

George said, "So they're disconnected and disorganized. Let's compare that to Chantilly. Are all of these areas, education, workforce development, communication, family, and the others, disconnected and disorganized in Chantilly?

Leonard said, "I wouldn't have said so a few months ago, but with what we know now, I'd have to say 'yes'."

"I agree," said McKenzie.

George said, "OK, Dr. Glenn's presentation told us about the movement from the countryside into cities, and the resulting disconnect from those local communities. But remember, the people who moved from those communities didn't just disconnect from the communities; they dismantled the bonds of social interactions that were part of their emotional, mental, physical, and spiritual food supply. That disconnect not only affected education, but it also affected everything else that constitutes a human support system. So, part of what we want to do tonight is organize and connect everything as much as we can. In the months to come, we'll figure out how to map these connections and get a snapshot of the whole community and its quantifiable human support assets. I'm having my graduate students do some work in this area now, using technology typically used for physical infrastructures. We have more to look at in that area."

George stepped up to the right hand side of the board, drew six circles in a circle, and labeled them 'Media,' 'Health,' 'Education,' 'Community,' 'Business,' and 'Government.' In the middle of the circle of circles, he drew a seventh circle, labeled 'Values, Vision, & Process.' Then he drew lines connecting the seven circles, stepped back, pointed to his diagram and said, "OK. I've given this a lot of thought over the years, and have talked with both of you and with many others, in Chantilly and out.

"These six categories include all the areas of difficulty and all the stakeholders in finding a solution."

McKenzie asked, "Where does the Chronicle fit, in business or media?"

George grinned and said, "They're not exclusive categories, but descriptions of identity and activity."

George turned to Leonard, waved at the board and asked, "Where would you put Terra Waste Management?"

"It's a business."

"That's its identity. But, where do you get your health coverage?"

"Terra's health plan."

"Uh huh. And where did Alice take Bruce that time he broke his foot during soccer practice?"

"Chantilly Hospital."

"So you also get healthcare from a community hospital run by the county government. Two of my grandkids were born there. Did you know it's a teaching hospital? The college nursing program trains nurses there."

McKenzie said, "So the hospital is an education center too."

George nodded and said, "Yes, it's all interconnected. The problem is, each of these areas, and each group within these areas, has their own little fragmented vision, and their own way of doing things." George pointed to the left side of the board and said, "They're not connected or aligned by a common vision. How can they be, when the individuals who make them up are so disconnected from their communities and out of touch with each other?"

"But, in order to truly work together for mutual benefit, these categories have to see themselves as part of a single interconnected group.

Chapter 14

George tapped his diagram with the marker and said, "These connections represent the contribution provided to the whole by each of these categories. 'Media' contributes the product of its function, 'Health' contributes, and so do 'Education,' 'Community,' 'Business,' and 'Government.' Each of these contributes something. But, in order for that contribution to be a benefit to the whole, that contribution must be in alignment with the values, vision, and process of the whole community."

Leonard frowned and said, "I don't quite see what you mean."

"Well, you probably don't know this, but the first European immigrants to this area were Germans. They built the first homes, church—First Lutheran, downtown—city hall, and newspaper. That first paper, the signs on the stores, and just about everything else, was in German.

"Of course, being in America, English speakers soon began moving into town. The new citizens put up their own church, Saint Paul's Presbyterian, and started their own paper, the Daily Chronicle.

"Naturally, for a while, because of the communication barrier, there were almost two communities. There were misunderstandings, different visions for the town, and mistrust between the German and English speakers. But as their ability to communicate grew, the misunderstandings disappeared, and they slowly became a single community.

"So, the ability to communicate easily meant everyone could be on the same page when it came time for celebrations, government policy changes, and, everything else. But, over time, as people began to acquire individualized communication tools, with information and programming that were not linked to the local community coming into their homes, they stopped paying close attention to local news. They began to lose touch with the pulse of their neighborhoods, with the people who governed and conducted local business."

"Yes, McKenzie?"

"But after World War II, it fell apart again, like Dr. Glenn said, as families moved from rural to urban communities, and we were left with disconnected disorder again. And as our communication on community issues became fragmented, people became less involved in local life. Young people especially became more and more concerned about, and identified with, the images they saw on the new media."

George said, "Yes, but we have to be careful here. I'm *not* suggesting we punish the messenger. The media corporations, electronic communications—television, DVDs, videogames, iPods, the 'net'—have super-developed ways of delivering a message. They're not the problem. The problem is that the message they deliver is disconnected from the values of the broader community, and thus it has a very disconnecting effect on the members of that community, especially our young people."

George noticed that Leonard was frowning and asked, "What's the matter, Leonard?"

"Well, a couple things. As someone who uses marketing technologies in a big way to grow my business, I want to explore the point about the 'message'. But, I also wonder if we have a similar concept about communication in 'integration' and 'alignment'."

McKenzie asked, "How do 'integration' and 'alignment' relate to communication? Are you talking systems again?"

"Well no, not just systems. To me, 'communication' means sharing information so that everyone has a common sense of where we're headed and how we're doing along the way, and can make timely and rational business decisions. The sharing is about ensuring that everyone sees the same information at the same time and understands it the same way.

"The systems are the pipeline for that information. We've worked hard to put in communications systems that move information quickly, efficiently, and almost seamlessly, and developed tools that display that information so we all understand it in the same way. This involves a lot of system interfaces—phone, fax, internet, LAN, etc., so we integrated them into an enterprise-wide communications system.

"In that context, 'alignment' is about ensuring that the information moved on that integrated system, that everything we do, is focused on and expresses our business strategy. We can't have the marketing department selling a product or service that we can't or won't deliver. And when they do sell a product, our production team has to know about it and be ready to deliver it on time and on budget. So we have to interact with our suppliers and make sure they'll have what we'll need when we'll need it.

"So, that's my quick view on the relationship between 'communication' and 'integration' and 'alignment'."

McKenzie turned to George and said, "You know, as you were talking about the history of Chantilly and the language barrier, I thought of how often people have conversations in English, and don't really understand what the other person is saying."

Leonard nodded and replied, "When I'm overseas, using translators, it's never clear whether or not the translator really translates the words I've spoken into words that convey my meaning. So often there's an *illusion* of communication. Our discussions sometimes give me the same feeling, with me as a businessman and you as a journalist. We often seem to use the same words, but with different meanings, and we're using the same language. No wonder we have such a hard time aligning."

George nodded to McKenzie again and she said, "That's not quite what I mean. When you were talking about your integrated and aligned network, I saw wires and radio waves that allowed you to move information around your company. But, as a reporter, that's not what I do. My job in 'communications' is to share information by writing stories that put that information into context and convey meaning. I share the 'who, what, where, when' that makes information relevant to people. That 'relevant' information is carried over wires, printed in the paper, broadcast on the evening news, etc."

George said, "So communication is both. It's the integration of the messenger and the message, of the wires and the information. *That's* what communication is!"

With a glint in his eye, Leonard asked, "So what's it called when people talk face-to-face, without wires?"

George's brows crinkled and he said, "You know, I've never liked phones. Well, not phones per se, but talking with people on them. When we talk with someone face-to-face, there's a depth and breadth to it that phones just don't have. When we communicate in person, we also have visual feedback and cues, tactile contact like handshakes or hugs, body language, facial expressions, a host of cues that are missing over the phone. And in email or text messages, we don't even have vocal cues like intonation, pronunciation, enunciation, pace, and everything else.

"So, in a sense, while all these other methods enable us to communicate with each other over greater distances of space and time, they also make us more remote from each other, because none of them are as intimate as direct contact. And because they're less intimate, they're also more impersonal. It takes much more effort to have the same degree of intimate communication over a phone than it does in person. For instance, one can send a very personal message to someone by holding and caressing their hand, but it is much more difficult, and requires a great deal of skill, to convey the same degree and intensity of meaning over the phone. It takes even more skill, a great deal of training and experience, to deliver the same intensity as a simple caress via email or text messages."

McKenzie said, "And yet, our schools, our society, the way kids live and play, aren't training them how to communicate."

George nodded and said, "They have more and more methods of communicating, but less and less skill in communicating."

Leonard said, "That's one of our biggest problems, finding new hires with basic communication skills. They can all use a cell phone and a computer, but that doesn't do us any good, because they still can't convey precise, detailed, information. They have the tools but not the skills."

McKenzie replied, "But marketers know how to do that. The companies and products they represent account for millions and millions of dollars on the research and development of razor sharp visual and word messages that will help sell their products, carefully targeting their audience." That level of attention to crafting a message made it tough when I was a teacher to send home a flyer and even hope that it got seen, much less read."

George held up a hand, looked at them both and said, "So, we've defined the problem. What's the next step?" He turned to Leonard and said, "When we had a real challenge at Terra, we'd bring everyone together in a single room and work on it together."

Leonard shrugged and replied, "It's the only way to get everyone on the same page, to get them aligned."

"Right, but with as diverse a group as we're talking about, we can't just bring everyone together in a room. We need a process to get them interacting and working together. Now, the most effective process I've found to reach alignment is called 'Common Ground.' It's a process that's been used worldwide, by hundreds of communities and organizations, and it meets two goals at the same time.

"It helps large, diverse groups discover common values, purposes, and projects that are central to understanding critical issues, and...

"It enables people to describe a desired future together in words or ways that everyone understands, and forms the basis for their creating an action plan that moves them in that direction.

"It's especially useful for bringing people together from different economic, social, business, and educational backgrounds, just as we're talking about here.

"Another thing that would make it a good process for us is that no one needs training or expertise in it."

Leonard said, "The A.W.M.A.[4] has been discussing the growing workforce problem for the past few years. They've assembled experts, written papers, held conferences, and taken all sorts of actions with waste management companies across the country. They're having yet another conference this weekend. Now, how is 'common ground' any different?"

McKenzie asked, "We've already agreed that we're talking about a fundamental change?"

"Right," Leonard replied, "That's one of the phases."

"Phases?" asked McKenzie.

"Right," Leonard responded, "One of the things I learned early in my career was that when building a

---

[4] American Waste Management Association

team, it goes through four distinct phases."

"And those are?" McKenzie asked.

"Well, the first phase is 'forming', as we've been doing the past few weeks. It's when we really don't know each other, tend to be very polite, and don't put the hard issues on the table.

"Phase two is the 'storming' phase, where politeness disappears. Things can get a bit ugly, but with the right intent, people really put issues on the table, let you know how they see things. It's here that people develop a common understanding of what things look like, so that the team can then sort out the way forward."

"Phase three is called 'norming'. It's where the members of the team reach alignment about what words mean, and reach an understanding of each other's background, perspective, and motivation.

"The fourth phase is called 'performing'. That's when the team is aligned and can get something done."

George asked, "And where would you place us?"

Leonard responded, "Well, we're emerging from phase two. We've all agreed that the issue of future workforce needs is much broader than just Terra, and are committed to cooperating on solving it."

George nodded and said, "Since we're going to work on this together, we need to discuss how we approach the issue."

Leonard stared out the window and said, "For me, it's all about helping people achieve the potential that we all have. Often we don't see it, or know what we can achieve, but that potential is still there."

McKenzie raised her brows in surprise, but Leonard merely smiled.

Leonard continued, saying, "One of the things that attracted me to Chantilly was that it felt like a really nice place to live and finish raising our family. What I brought with me was my family, my experience as a leader, and a set of tools and skills that I picked up before arriving.

"Right away, as I began doing my job, I had to help everyone in the organization understand my view of a leader,

that true leaders are the ones who provide a vision about where we want to go,

apply the necessary resources to make it happen,

provide a map that helps everyone know where we are along the journey, and finally,

leaders break down the barriers that stop their employees' forward progress.

"When employees know that leaders are there to help, their level of commitment and capability goes up dramatically. So, my view of leadership is that first and foremost the leader must model the values, provide the vision, and take care of those who turn the vision into reality.

"The *Merchants of Cool* video hit me hard, because it showed that many of us, as leaders, aren't communicating a compelling vision to our youth about a future that isn't up for sale, but that can be achieved through personal initiative. We've abdicated that responsibility to the marketplace.

"Instead of businesses and organizations competing to draw our youth's time and attention to 'cool' goods and services, maybe we should work to give our future workforce a vision of their potential, of who they are and what they could be, and help them learn the skills and capabilities they'll need in order to fulfill that potential.

"Now, I don't know exactly how to reach the kids who will be our future workforce, or how to create the vision that they'll find compelling, other than to use the same media they do. I've got to get more insights into how messages are developed. But, what I do know how to do, is to bring a group of adults together and help facilitate a discussion that results in a common vision for that particular group, and to put in place a strategy, structure, set of resources, skill set, staff, and shared values that will allow that vision to be achieved.

Leonard gazed at McKenzie and said, "You know, when I was studying for my MBA, I learned about an individual who had the same last name as your first name. He had a theory that in order for an organization to maximize its potential for success, it needed to have seven key items integrated and aligned. That '7S' model[5] provides a comprehensive guide to analyzing the culture and behavior of an organization. It provides a framework for aligning with and agreeing on the seven key elements. Let me show you what it looks like, because I believe seeing the concept on the board provides a powerful statement about what it really means."

George nodded and said, "I remember your discussions on that. My sense is that the 'common ground' model results in where to go, and the 7S model helps ensure that all elements of the organization are aligned to achieve the future state."

Leonard stepped up to the left side of the board, began erasing it and said, "I'll use Terra as an example. The shared vision for Terra includes a statement that an important part of our measure of success is 'meeting customer expectations.' The way we've operationalized that part of the strategy is to ensure employees make the call on field decisions."

"'Operationalized?'" asked McKenzie.

"Oh, sorry. Um... made a normal part of our activities.

---

[5] A framework for analyzing and improving organizational effectiveness

"Now, we use a set of guidelines. If an employee steps out of bounds—what we as leaders believe is the right step—we hold an 'after action' meeting that includes peer employees, and talk about the circumstances and decision. What we don't do is penalize the employee for making what he or she thought was the right decision. Implementing 'after action' meetings requires alignment of our leadership style, organizational structure, systems that authorize work, and selection of the right staff for field assignments."

George noticed the time, and the blinking red lights on Leonard's phone and said, "Leonard, this is important, but I think it's time we begin wrapping up for today.

"What we've shared is important, and I suggest we take a little time to consider it, and meet again in a couple days. In that time, those of us who aren't familiar with some of what we discussed, such as 'common ground' and '7S', can look into those, so we have a better grounding for our next meeting."

McKenzie said, "I'll round up more data and information to help us build a solid picture of what's happening."

As she stuck her materials in her briefcase, McKenzie took one last glance at the board, turned to Leonard and said, "You know, I thought corporate executives like you spent a lot of time pontificating and were pretty hard for ordinary people like me to talk with. I'm not sure how many there are like you, but I'm sure glad we finally met."

Leonard grinned, stuck out his hand, and as they shook, said, "Well, McKenzie, I always thought you were so hard on us because you were just out for a 'story'. But seeing your passion and desire to help has changed my view of you. I'm actually looking forward to working together. Let's all meet again when I get back from the A.W.M.A. conference."

Chapter 14

After work, Leonard set his luggage into the trunk, slammed it shut, and walked back to the house. On the way, he noticed the limp, brown, carcasses of blossoms clinging to Alice's prize roses. He strode through the house and out back, where Alice sat, watching Bruce playing Frisbee with his dog.

Leonard gently laid his hand on Alice's left shoulder, and she rose to receive his hug. As they embraced, Alice said, "I'd forgotten how precious those hours were in the middle of the day. Now that I'm arranging his routine, and volunteering at his school, all my time is taken up again."

Leonard replied, "I wish there was more I could do."

Alice said, "This isn't one of those solutions they sell, it's one you have to live.

"By the way, Dr. Gedissman's office called. They're ready for our next appointment."

Leonard asked, "Is it urgent?"

Alice replied, "No. He just has a new treatment he wants to tell us about. He sounded pretty excited."

Leonard said, "Give Jane a call and she'll arrange it. I'll call you when I get to the conference."

Chapter 15

Assembling Facts and Data

"Life shrinks or expands in proportion to one's courage."
Anaias Nin

Chapter 15

Leonard lifted his napkin to his mouth, coughed out a piece of chicken gristle and then demanded, "What do you base *that* on?"

It was the second evening of the annual A.W.M.A. Conference, and Leonard had four chance dinner companions. He'd met so many new people that he couldn't remember who everyone was, but their nametags identified them as 'Dr. Michael Hernandez, President, American Science Teachers' Association,' 'Gill Chandler, Reporter, National Waste Management Journal,' 'Congressman Joe Delaney,' and 'Larry Spandle, Director, Academy of Engineering.'

They'd reached the stage of the meal where the food was becoming secondary to the conversation. Larry, trying to look thoughtful while chewing, but failing, swallowed and replied, "The Chinese spin their numbers. Besides, the competition for positions in American engineering schools is way up."

Leonard snorted and said, "But nationally 43% of Engineering graduates are foreign born, and most of those don't stay in the U.S."

Still looking at Leonard, Larry nodded toward Congressman Delaney and replied, "So get Congress to increase the funding of Science and Engineering programs, so we can expand the programs to meet domestic demand."

Leonard replied, "Funding isn't the real problem. America spends over $500 billion on K through 12, more per student than any other nation, yet our students continue to fall behind in nearly every measure of academic achievement."

Dr. Hernandez put his spoonful of peas on his plate and said, "Because there aren't enough teachers, especially in math and science. Across the country it's getting increasingly difficult to find qualified teachers, especially for middle and high school science and math. Over the next five years, we'll need 200,000 more teachers, and we don't know where they're coming from."

Leonard nodded and asked, "Why so many?"

Dr. Hernandez put his now-cold peas down again and said, "Well, there's the usual attrition, of course. But a lot of them are retiring. The average age is about 50."

Leonard replied, "I'm having similar problems," then turned to Larry and asked, "What did you mean about the Chinese spinning their numbers?"

Larry swallowed a bite of peach cobbler and said, "Our statistics only include full Engineers, four year degrees or better. Theirs include 'Engineers' with two-year certificates. They pad the numbers to make it look like they have more engineers than they really have."

Leonard frowned and said, "But that's an academic definition of 'engineer'. As a businessman, I need a practical, functional definition."

Dr. Hernandez frowned and asked, "What do you mean by 'functional'?

Leonard signaled the waiter and asked for a raw egg. Then he nodded to Gill and said, "Last spring the Journal published an article on one of our Chinese jobs."

Gill swallowed and said, "Waste water purification, wasn't it, built around your Aguilera Sonic Scrubbers?"

"Right. A lot of the Chinese 'Engineers' on that job had the two year certificates Larry mentioned, but they could still do the job we hired them for. Now, we got that contract because we've built similar plants in the U.S. and elsewhere. However, in the U.S. we find that so many new full Engineers, with the 'right' four-year degree, can't do the job. They have plenty of book knowledge, but don't know how to apply that to real world situations, and that's what I need. Because of that knowledge-skills gap, it was a lot harder to find Engineers for domestic contracts than it was for the Chinese."

Larry frowned in puzzlement and said, "They don't have the right training?"

Leonard shook his head and said, "It's not just an education problem; more teachers, bigger programs, more money, none of that will fix it."

The waiter arrived with Leonard's egg. He accepted it, held it up and said, "Look, I'm going to give you a simple engineering problem. Set this egg on end, on the table, without letting it touch anything but the table."

Leonard set the egg on the middle of the table and waited. Gill tried spinning it, like a top, but each attempt flopped. Larry and Dr. Hernandez tried balancing it, but it immediately tipped over. The others gave up before trying, and then all of them looked expectantly at Leonard. Leonard picked up the egg with the slender end up, tapped the fat end on the table so it dented, let go, and left it standing there. Leonard nodded to the egg and said, "It's not how *much* they know, it's what they can *do* with what they know."

Larry looked puzzled and asked, "How's that different? Now that we know the solution, we can all do it."

Leonard shook his head slightly and asked, "Are you saying that what it takes to be an engineer is knowing how things are done?"

Larry nodded and said, "You have to have the right information and know how to process that information. But yes, that's what a good engineering program does."

Leonard looked at the Congressman and asked, "Congressman, how would you define 'education'?"

Congressman Delaney finished sipping his coffee, grinned affably and said, "Well... Thomas Jefferson said, 'The purpose of education is to create young citizens with knowing heads and loving hearts.'"

Leonard gazed around the table and said, "Suppose you have a problem that no one has ever seen before? Someone has to think up the answer the first time, and that's what I need. I need people, not just engineers, who can think creatively on their feet. And it's not just me. Business and industry is getting increasingly technical, facing new challenges. We all need people capable of meeting those challenges, and most of the kids entering the workforce just can't do that.

By the time McKenzie reached Terra Waste, the worst of the storm had passed, and the last of the rain was flowing out of the parking lot. Grateful for the escape from a drenching, she popped her trunk, unfolded her handcart, stacked two file boxes on it, and wheeled them toward the main entrance.

When McKenzie opened the outer door to Leonard's office, she found him on his way out. Leonard immediately leaped forward and held open the door, while McKenzie wheeled in the boxes. When she was inside, he said, "George is here. I'll be right back, biological break." and left.

Jane opened the inner door for McKenzie, and held it while she wheeled the boxes into Leonard's inner office. George was seated at the small conference table. He started to rise when he saw her, realized that she didn't need his help with the door, and that he couldn't lift heavy boxes yet, and sat back down.

McKenzie grinned at him and asked, "How's your back?"

"It'll be all right, but my chiropractor says I can't wrestle Dusty anymore."

McKenzie opened the top box, began pulling out

Chapter 15

folders and documents and said, "But you can still watch him play."

George's brows crinkled and he said, "You know, that's what grandparents used to do."

"What?"

"Watch the children. The men would be out hunting while the women gathered, or later the men would work the fields while the women cared for the homes, but the grandparents watched the children. We used to teach them, too. The grandfathers would teach the boys how to be men, and the grandmothers taught the girls how to be women. It was one of the greatest breakthroughs in human evolution. It freed up the parents to do a thousand other things—hunt, gather, and prepare food, and make clothing or shelter. But we don't have that any more, not like we used to."

"Well, a lot of parents dump the kids on the grandparents to raise. Did Dr. Glenn mention grandparenting? That sounds like another effect of the 1946 baby boom."

"Which, the watching or the dumping?"

"Either."

"I don't think he did, but children aren't the only ones who lost their place and purpose."

McKenzie was almost done organizing her materials when the door opened and Leonard stepped in. He glanced at the folders on the table and asked. "So where do we start?"

Still holding a manila folder, McKenzie turned to him and asked, "How much time do we have?"

"This is my last meeting today."

McKenzie nodded, and the three of them found places at the table. McKenzie slid a final folder between two others, nodded toward George while looking at Leonard and asked, "Why can't you find replacements for your technical leaders like George?"

"If I had an easy answer to that, this would be a short meeting. But you both know how difficult that is to articulate. I suppose the biggest problem is that most people just don't understand the problem. During a break at the A.W.M.A. Conference, I had dinner with four people who could have a tremendous influence on education thought around the country. They all cared deeply about what they did, but none of them had a complete picture of what's going on with today's youth or had a solution to the workforce problem. Oh, each of them had their ideas, but they were limited to their own, narrow, perspective."

George asked, "How so?"

"When I tried to explain the situation at Terra, in specific, or the problems of business and industry in general, they just didn't get it. They were so focused on their own little piece of the problem that they didn't see the rest. It was too big or it made their heads hurt. They wanted a silver bullet they could take back and implement today. In other words, their thinking styles are actually mirrored by the young people, who want a solution right now. They'd talk about their education programs, and the benefits of those, but none of them knew what the others were doing, and none of their programs will help *us*. They weren't the only ones I spoke with, but they were typical."

McKenzie said, "Sounds discouraging."

"More 'disheartening;' I was already discouraged."

George asked, "Why wouldn't their programs be of help?"

"Well, it's not that there was anything wrong with them. I wouldn't know. But... George, you know how our plants work, and McKenzie, your paper has one of those big presses? It's like each of those programs was a piece of a manufacturing or printing process, but none of them knew about the others, so they weren't set up to work together. They weren't working on the same problem; their output wasn't compatible; and they were all competing instead of working together."

George nodded and said, "Just a huge, noisy mess with lots of activity but nothing changing."

Leonard nodded, a bit dispiritedly and said, "You'd have been proud of me, McKenzie. I've gotten much better at communicating, the way you mean it, but that didn't help.

"Why not?"

"Well, whenever I described the problem to a group, someone would usually come up to me afterwards and say, 'I understand what you mean, and I have a program for that'!"

George said, "They can't see past their own piece of it."

"Yes. And of course everyone thinks that *their* program is *best*."

George said, "We'll have to be very careful. Egos could be a major problem, and this will only work if the major... stakeholders... all work together.

Leonard said, "I serve on several nonprofit boards, and getting results from volunteers is different from paid staff. Many years ago, I was the tribal leader for my band, and it was very different from my business roles. When it was time to make decisions, every member of the tribe got a chance to express their opinion and to participate in deciding how to implement decisions. 'We the people' decided.

"Too often, we business leaders think we need to make all of the decisions, when our role really should be about finding the best people, sharing the vision for the business, putting in place tools to ensure we all know where we are, and then making sure we can do what we said we would do.

"This is why finding the right replacement for George and the other retirees is critical for Terra. We can teach people new skills, but they have to have the right attitude, core skill set, and behaviors before they show up at the door."

McKenzie said, "I'd include 'character' and 'values' for the public service sector—like teaching. But think I know what you mean. For years, as a teacher and then as a reporter, I've watched workers struggling to keep up with rapid changes in job requirements and technology. But, some do very well while others struggle. I've come to learn that self-esteem, derived from having achieved something with your own hands, is a big factor in whether or not people are willing to risk doing something new. Having the 'right attitude' is too often touted as being important, but attitude is a way of externalizing self-confidence so it still comes back to having self-esteem.

"The other important determining factor is what I call 'capacity for learning new things'. You may recall I have quite a fascination for mapping things, and lately I've taken up studying the pathways that are laid down in the brain, like lines on a map, when we're infants and learning to creep and crawl. These pathways become the critical connections between synapses in the brain and enhancing its capacity for intelligent activity."

"McKenzie, why haven't I ever heard of anything like that before?" Leonard asked.

"My best guess? It's not commercial enough. Creeping and crawling are best done with no props and no interference, only the loving eyes of a caregiver. Hard to make money on it."

"We'll have to discuss that later. Bruce's doctor has been talking about something like that, but I didn't understand what the implications were for him. Thanks for bringing it up."

Chapter 15

"You're welcome, maybe we can talk about it later."

McKenzie said, "Anyway, I used to think executives at your level didn't value people except as expendable resources, easily replaced cogs in a giant machine. I know that's a stereotype, but I've run into it so much that it's hard not to believe there's some truth in it."

Leonard replied, "Unfortunately, there *is* an element of truth to that, perhaps more than we would like to admit. A business makes money by efficiently moving things along. Otherwise, your competition will overrun you. This often includes having to make short-term decisions that create long-term problems, such as laying off people to save money when things are slow only to create long-term inefficiencies in getting things done."

McKenzie nodded and said, "Through the loss of 'tribal knowledge' held by the laid off workers."

Leonard replied, "That's one example, yes. In fact, George is an excellent example of that, and it's part of why we haven't been able to replace him. Not only is he a great scientist, but he's a leader among both his peers and subordinates, and he's been around so long he can sense the ebb and flow, the cycles, of the business. You can't replace that overnight, it takes decades of experience."

"Cycles?"

George nodded and said, "Every business has to keep an eye on the market, on the changes in technology and product demand. Something is always coming into demand, while some things are going out. To keep a business healthy, you have to watch a lot of things outside your business that affect your business, and when the market changes, you have to see it coming long before it is really a threat to your business, or your life for that matter, and adapt with it. A lot of young hires think that they can predict changes or trends by just punching numbers into a computer, but that won't work. In order to move with the flow of change, you have to be part of it, move into and within it. If you sit back and watch, it'll just pass you by."

McKenzie said, "Which is where communication skills come in."

George said, "And 'identification', the ability to place yourself in the 'shoes' of another person and appreciate what they think and feel. Kids today are spending so much time staring at screens—television, computer, game, cell—that they're not developing basic associative skills, the ability to identify or communicate with real people."

McKenzie said, "That's a very interesting way to describe what's happening to young people, even after they've supposedly gotten an education, and it relates to all this paperwork I've brought.

"When we first heard Dr. Glenn talk, I wanted to see how real it was here in Chantilly. I thought maybe that a small city like ours wouldn't be affected as much. Of course, I knew about our test scores, but I didn't know the stats on our teen pregnancies, suicides, and drug and alcohol abuse. But I checked. And you know what? Chantilly followed the same pattern as the rest of the country. Everything Dr. Glenn said was as true here as everywhere else, and I have the statistics to prove it."

Leonard sat up a little straighter and asked, "How much have things changed?"

McKenzie said, "Well, they've changed a lot. Except for a few islands of excellence, like George's kids, our young people are increasingly unprepared for the future."

Leonard snorted and said, "You mean our $250,000 grant for new computers for the schools didn't 'dramatically' change their education?"

McKenzie shook her head and said, "Using a computer is a skill, Leonard. Typing on a keyboard and staring at a monitor doesn't build growing minds the way

Chapter 15

playing outside does."

"'Growing minds'? So, what does?"

"Well, part of the problem is confusion between basic capabilities and skills. Let me show you some of the data that I've collected. You know I've been reporting on business, education, and community issues for years. Like you, I've struggled to make sense of much of what I've seen and heard, because so much of it isn't related."

George interjected, "Doesn't *appear* to be related."

McKenzie nodded and said, "Right. As a community, we used to be more in touch with each other and with what was going on in Chantilly. Back then, an article in the Chronicle on the largest business in town would bring in dozens of letters from ordinary citizens. But now, when I report on Terra Waste, most folks miss the implications. They don't feel a connection between themselves, Chantilly, and Terra. We're living such fractured, 'niched' lives that we don't know, or much care, what people are doing in our own back yard."

George moved his gaze from McKenzie to Leonard and said, "This is a very important point, which we'll have to explore in detail at some point in the future. If people don't care about their local relationships, their community, there are two main reasons for that. One is a breakdown in the connections between people, the other is a waning of the ability to *see* those connections. Both are disastrous for the community, and the latter, the inability to see relationships, is part of the difficulty you're having in finding new personnel for Terra."

When George finished, McKenzie turned back to Leonard and said, "We can go into the details of that later, but I want to be very clear that what I have to share with you is, I think, at the heart of what will either catapult Chantilly into the future or lead to its decline and death. The difference depends on what we do about it as a community.

"Now, I haven't really been able to order this by priority. Some of it you probably already know, and some of it you don't. I hope, that at the end of this meeting, we'll have a basic set of key ideas that we all agree on and can use as the foundation for our teamwork. Oh, and feel free to jump in with comments or questions anytime.

"I've covered a lot of business stories, and I get lots of contradictory information in both research and anecdotes. It's often like your experience at the A.W.M.A. convention. Everyone sees things from their own perspective and comes to entirely different conclusions. The result is a mixed bag of 'hard' facts and soft opinions that I have to sort through to find the story. And this happened every time I tried to cover a company, any company, that was having trouble finding people with the skills they need."

"How many?"

"How many companies? Well, as far as I can tell, just about all of them in Chantilly. I've looked at everything from big companies like Terra to neighborhood hair salons. It doesn't seem to matter what kind of business it is, or how large. They're all having trouble finding people with the skills they need. Local population statistics show that there are plenty of people in Chantilly who are the right age for these employers, but the businesses don't hire them."

Leonard nodded and said, "The skills problem again."

"Right. It's the same problem. The potential employees don't have the skills the businesses need. Now, there are a number of reasons for that, but I've identified two basic issues. One is the... 'narrowing' of the skill set of youth entering the workforce. The other is the changing skill sets needed by employers. It used to be that someone could learn a skill set, enter a profession, and practice that same skill set for their entire career. That hardly ever happens anymore. Now, in order to be marketable as a employee, you have to keep your skill set constantly up to date."

George said, "Lifelong learning."

"Yes. Now, as a reporter one of my jobs is to attempt to write a story with a beginning, a middle, and an end—whether I'm covering a person, place, or event—and provide readers with balanced perspective.

"Not unbiased."

"There's always a bias. In the first place, being a reporter requires having a perspective. And then everyone you speak to has theirs, so I have to integrate it all into a story, one that can be shared, understood, and embraced by our readers.

Leonard said, "Sounds like something George said."

"We've talked about this a lot."

Leonard stood, walked to the white board, reached for one of the markers and said, "Okay, let's put some of those facts up."

McKenzie asked, "Wouldn't it be easier for me to just keep notes and write it up later?"

George shook his head and said, "No, because we're not really trying to 'organize' information."

Leonard smiled and nodded and McKenzie asked, "We're not?"

George replied, "We're looking for the underlying order, the basic principles that produce the effects we're seeing."

"But how do you know...

"Because we live in an ordered universe. The information you've 'brought to the table' will help expand our picture of what's going on. What we need to do is look at that picture, find the story, and find the plot or order behind the story. From the order, we can determine the basic principles involved, and once we know the basic principles, then we'll be able to use those principles to 'revise the plot' or write a new story.?

"So, we're looking for a 'happy ending'?"

George grinned artfully and said, "More of an open-ended continuation, of the 'and they lived happily ever after' variety. And since we're looking for relationships, it's easier if we do so as a related group."

"OK."

Leonard asked, "What about all the others who are part of this problem? When do they come in?"

George replied, "Well, they come in when their stories bring them to that point. All this information McKenzie has, it's pieces of their stories, right? We've got this," George reached picked up one of one of McKenzie's folders, pulled out a couple of news clippings and said, "what... story about unfilled internship jobs worth thousands of dollars. Increasing demands for highly trained technical people, but increasing unemployment. Continued decline in high school test scores, while college SAT scores are at an all time high. At this point, all of this is unrelated information, and none of it seems to make sense, but it will when we put it together into a larger story."

And with that, with the aid of George's advice and direction, Leonard started writing what McKenzie and he knew on the board. Five hours later the rain had stopped, the sky was clearing, and a full moon shone so bright it cast a pale rainbow. McKenzie and Leonard had papered the wall with copies of charts they'd created on the white board, and like proud artists admiring their creation, they stopped and gazed over their work.

Silently, Leonard joined George back at the table, and slumped down in his chair. He looked up studied the walls carefully, absorbing the meaning and messages they'd created. McKenzie stood back, sensed an

Chapter 15

opportunity for a break, and slipped out.

When she returned, she found George watching and making suggestions as Leonard dashed back and forth, moving charts around the wall. Finally, he stepped back, gazed at the result with a satisfied grin and said, "I'll be right back."

Leonard left, passed through his empty outer office into the now quiet hall, and returned a few minutes later with a pot of tea. The three of them sat in silence as they enjoyed a cup, but it was clear that the wheels were spinning in their minds as they reflected on the potential of their creation—the outline of a story.

They contemplated it for a few minutes, quietly sipping their tea, before McKenzie finally asked, "What do you think?"

Leonard chuckled and said, "We have to share this with a few others, move the process forward, test it out, and see if it flies."

McKenzie asked, "What do you mean 'process'?"

Leonard replied, "Well, it's time to share this with other 'stakeholders,' to get their side of the story. After all, this isn't a story about you, me, or them. It's about a shared vision that we can all use in creating the future. And if we're all going to support it and stand by it, they have to help create it, kind of like the way things started with our Constitution. So, who should we share it with first?"

McKenzie asked, "Are we ready for that? Stories are supposed to have a beginning, a middle, and an end, but this has no end. It looks like it has only a beginning and a bit of a middle."

George set his tea down, turned to McKenzier said, "What we're envisioning is a process for creating the future, and because it's a process, the story doesn't have an end."

McKenzie nodded and said, "So the 'who' is everyone, the 'what' is the healing or transformation of our
society, the 'where' is Chantilly, at least for now, 'when'
is the future, and the 'how' is the process."

Leonard said, "The 'who' includes the individuals
and institutions that shape and influence the future
workforce... the pipeline."

McKenzie responded, "In my world, that's everybody."

Leonard said, "You're right. It's the *system*, the
whole system. It includes everybody."

McKenzie replied, "I'll create an outline from my
notes and email it to both of you."

With heads nodding and smiles born of satisfaction,
the three gathered their things, shut the door to Leonard's office, and walked in near silence into the cooling
night air beneath the shining moon.

Chapter 16

Working Collaboratively to Build Integrated Solutions

"We have the power to shape the civilization that we want. But we need your will, your labor, your hearts, if we are to build that kind of society. Those who came to this land sought to build more than just a new country. They sought a new world. So I have come here today to your campus to say that you can make their vision our reality. So let us from this moment begin our work so that in the future men will look back and say: It was then, after a long and weary way, that man turned the exploits of his genius to the full enrichment of his life."

Lyndon B. Johnson, "Great Society" speech, 1964

Seeking the Soul of Commerce

Chapter 16

Later that night, while he was sleeping, Leonard received the following:

From: McKenzieJ@ChantillyChronicle.com
To: Leonard@TerraWaste.com,
GeorgeA@Chantilly.net
Time: 11:42 P.M.

Leonard and George,
I've condensed the outline into the following main points:

The Challenge

It's not a labor shortage but a *skill* shortage, skills and personal traits.

Different groups speak the language of success using a different set of words, but we must adopt a common terminology if we are to be successful

The community is responsible for creating *citizens* of the future who are also capable of being the *workers* of the future

Schools alone are not responsible for creating capable future citizens

There is a misalignment between what is required to be taught in school and what is needed for success in life, including in the workplace

Education doesn't begin when kids go to school and it can't end when they leave school

Fixing schools alone does not solve the problem

Media must be part of the solution

No one is to blame... circumstances have changed.

More programs are not the answer

The Vision

We are creating a vision of alignment, integration and the necessary leadership to make that vision become reality

The vision must be a shared vision such that everyone will want to help create it and see the role they play in making it reality

It takes many groups and stakeholders (government, education, business, media, health, community organizations) working together to turn the vision into reality

The Process

Clarify the Purpose or Goal
Move that Goal into Appearance
Compare the result with the Purpose
Reclarify the Purpose

I definitely need feedback on this, especially the "Process" part. How close is it, what needs to be changed, expanded, who will we share it with and when?

McKenzie

From: Leonard@TerraWaste.com
To: McKenzieJ@ChantillyChronicle.com,
GeorgeA@Chantilly.net
Time: 5:05 A.M.

Morning McKenzie!

Well, I see you didn't waste any time; must be the reporter's drive to get the story out.

Your summary is quite good. The basic problem is that our requirement for highly skilled people is increasing, yet the supply of those skills seems to be decreasing. There are three basic ways to deal with this:

Increase skills like critical thinking in education—this includes K through 16, postgraduate education, and other skills-based programs.

Keep workers around longer by developing worker retention approaches. At Terra we are developing a number of worker retention policies, eliminating mandatory retirement, increasing vacations and decreasing hours for elder workers, and other methods of encouraging our older, more experienced employees to remain with us.

Improve the skills of those already in the workforce. This would, of course, include life-long learning and skills development programs of many kinds.

Regards,
Leonard

From: GeorgeA@Chantilly.net
To: McKenzieJ@ChantillyChronicle.com,
Leonard@TerraWaste.com
Time: 7:38 A.M.

Morning McKenzie and Leonard:
I see yesterday's meeting stimulated a lot of insights.

Leonard, I'm glad to see you applying the production process analogy in that way. I know, of course, that you're aware of the dangers of "objectifying" people, and as long as we steer clear of that, it will be very useful. How far have you gone with the process analogy at this point?

McKenzie, are you following this?

From: McKenzieJ@ChantillyChronicle.com
To: GeorgeA@Chantilly.net,
Leonard@TerraWaste.com

Time: 8:15 A.M.

George, I'm not sure. How does comparing the problem with industrial production help?

From: Leonard@TerraWaste.com
To: McKenzieJ@ChantillyChronicle.com,
GeorgeA@Chantilly.net
Time: 8:35 A.M.

McKenzie,
The production analogy enables us to apply the "systems" problem solving methods developed by industry.

As we've seen, technical industries everywhere are facing a crisis as significant percentages of seasoned and skilled workers prepare for retirement, with insufficient skilled replacements in the wings. There are growing concerns about what will happen if current industry leaders don't act now and the pipeline for future workers runs empty.

Because today's community, educational, government, health, media, and business systems are not fully aligned, young people coming into the workforce do not have the skills that any of those portions of society need. You saw the developing skills problem in media well over a decade ago, and I've been forced to recognize it more recently in business and industry, but it's pervasive. We, all of us as a society, are not preparing people to enter the future workforce equipped with the innovative and creative thinking abilities that will be desperately needed in the future.

Technology-based industries are experiencing this especially acutely, because many of our needs are very quantifiable, very measurable. But it's not just our prob-

Chapter 16

lem; it is everyone's problem. Because Terra has well developed integrated systems thinking processes, it can and must take on its share of the responsibility to help create and implement a new vision of the future for itself and Chantilly.

Regards,

Leonard

From: GeorgeA@Chantilly.net
To: McKenzieJ@ChantillyChronicle.com,
Leonard@TerraWaste.com
Time: 10:15 A.M.

McKenzie,

Sorry to take so long to get back to you. Donna called me in to breakfast (oatmeal and fresh fruit) and then Elizabeth brought Dusty over.

Remember, it's all about sharing our stories so they become *one* story. In a sense, systems management is a way of looking at a situation, finding the story line or plot of that story, and then retelling the story so that it works.

Now, the first step in telling any story (in fiction more so than in news) is to decide on the goal or purpose of the story. In business and industry, the story is usually about making money. But for society as a whole, we could say that the story is about creating citizens of the future (who are also capable of being the *workers* of the future).

Then, where in writing, you identify the conflicts (inner and outer) that must be faced and overcome by the characters, in business, you identify the systems constraints, or the bottlenecks that restrict production.

Where in writing, you decide how to use the conflicts to further the unfoldment of the story,

in business, you decide how to exploit the constraints.

Where in writing, everything else: character, setting, dialogue, action, etc., is secondary to exploiting the conflicts,

in business, you subordinate everything to the decision to exploit the constraints.

Where in writing, action, scene, plot, the characters, all move from conflict to conflict,

in business, everything moves from constraint to constraint. They are the most important part, the key, of the process.

Where in writing, resolving a conflict leads to or creates a new one, and one must then begin the conflict resolution process from the beginning,

in business, once a constraint has been broken, you go back to the beginning (keeping things moving so that inertia does not become or cause a system constraint).

I hope this helps. We should discuss it more when we get together again. We're going to need a clear "plot outline"—a goal statement, explanation of the current condition that clearly indicates in what ways that goal is not being met, and a clear explanation and theoretical outline of the process—that we can take to the larger community (I suggest via the Lyceum, as most of Chantilly's key decision makers are members).

Are both of you available tomorrow afternoon, same time as yesterday?

George

Chapter 17

Keeping the Focus on the Future

"There is nothing so powerful as an idea whose time has come."
Victor Hugo

Chapter 17

Donna called out, "Dear, Leonard's here!" and led him down the hall to the door of what was originally the family room, but had been George's home office and library since their children moved out. George's desk and bookshelves were still there and obviously in use, but new furnishings—a "play-house" assembled from cardboard boxes, foam balls, stuffed animals, toy tools, and picture books—suggested that it now doubled as their youngest grandchild's play room. Leonard was surprised to find that impression confirmed by the presence of Dusty, who, with McKenzie's help, was photographing a large LEGO® dinosaur.

George looked up from the paint-stained easel he was assembling and said, "Hi Leonard. Elizabeth has been delayed, so Dusty is going to play with us for a while." George turned toward Dusty and said, "Dusty, what do you say?"

Dusty paused to turn and wave and said, "H'lo Uncle Leonard. See what I made!"

Leonard smiled and exclaimed, "Wow, that's quite a project. What do you do with the photos?"

Dusty hopped over to a shelf, grabbed a portfolio with "Dusty's Inventions" printed on the cover. He hopped over to Leonard, thrust the folder at him and said, "Aunt McKenzie's helping me make this. Before I take something apart for the pieces, I take a picture of it, so I can remember it." He smiled broadly, and Leonard couldn't help but smile back.

Wanna see what I can do now?" asked Dusty.

"Sure!" Leonard replied.

Dusty hopped over to what looked like a playground ladder, stretched horizontally between two wooden step ladders. It was carefully anchored so it wouldn't move around, its rungs, wood dowels, were just fat enough for Dusty's hands, it was sized so Dusty's feet were never far from the ground, and some kind of workout padding covered the floor under and around it.

Leonard said, "Wow, what's all this stuff? Looks like Grandpa George has been redesigning playground equipment."

Dusty stood at one end of the ladder with his back to Leonard. He lowered his head to his chin, took a deep breath, turned to face the length of the ladder, and reached up so his fingers grasped the first rung. He swung out, grabbed the next rung, released the first, swung forward and grabbed the third. Dusty continued, gasping and grimacing, grasped each rung in turn and swinging down the entire length of the ladder.

Leonard grinned at Dusty's antics, curious about what George was doing.

Dusty reached the end of the ladder, hopped down,, stood for a moment in triumph and shrieked, "I did it! Did you see me Grandpa? I got all the way to the end. Yeah!"

"Come here, Son." said George. "That was terrific! See, I told you you were ready. I'm so proud of you!" With that, George gave his grandson a tight hug. Then Dusty trotted off to get some juice from his Grandma.

Leonard remained silent while they celebrated. Glancing around the room, he noticed a number of additional objects he hadn't seen before, including an arrangement of boards like a balance beam, and a big ball. When Dusty left, he asked, "What is all this stuff?"

"Well," George replied, "it's a long story, one you'll definitely want to know about. But I wanted to try some things with Dusty first to make sure they made sense. "

Leonard raised a brow and asked "And?"

"If this process works as well as it seems to, then we may well be looking at a significant 'root cause' for enhanced brain capacity among young children."

"Playground equipment? What does that have to do with 'brain capacity'?"

"Well, as far and McKenzie or I have been able to uncover, every child is born with the tendency to perform certain physical acts, to act out in specific ways. However, the people who are present at the birth and and engaged in the early life of the child alter many of the actions that a newborn and young child would take if left to move naturally. Adults tend to intervene constantly.

This appears to be a contributing part of the overall problem. You'd be in a better position to understand why if I outlined the things we do, just in this culture, that interrupt simple, natural acts. It's something we need to look at further. Some groups already have, and I'm just doing due diligence, trying some of their steps for myself."

Dusty returned at that point and George said, "I'll tell you much more about it as we go along. Is that okay?"

"Sure, it does look interesting, and fun. Is it productive so far?"

"Amazingly so."

"Great."

"Shall we move to our reason for being here now? Dusty, go find your chair."

Leonard grinned as he wondered how George was going to pull this off and asked, "What are we playing?"

Tightening a butterfly nut, George said, "The Alliance Game."

"It's like Hide 'n Seek, but with words." declared Dusty.

Leonard suppressed a chuckle. George caught his eye, nodded toward a stack of white plastic lawn chairs in a corner and asked, "Would you grab four of those?"

"Four?"

"Donna's joining us."

While Leonard set up the chairs, George placed a poster-sized drawing pad on the easel, set a handful of colored markers in the holder built into the easel and said, "We're almost ready. Oh, leave room there for Dusty's chair."

Donna brought in a tray with everyone's favorite brews and the mixed aroma of hot chocolate, coffee, warm milk, and a variety of spices. Dusty and McKenzie finished, and Dusty grabbed his own chair and began to drag it toward the others, but Donna said, "Carry it, Dear."

Dusty replied, "Yes, Nona," lifted his chair, and set it down in the space Leonard had left between George and Donna's chairs.

When they were all seated facing the easel, George turned to Dusty and said, "OK. Dusty, this is a game adults sometimes play. It's called 'The Alliance Process,' and it's a way of, well, getting together and discovering where you agree with each other."

"Agree about what?"

"What to do about a problem. You see, when there's a problem and people get together to talk about it, sometimes everyone has a different opinion on what the problem is and what needs to be done."

"Do they fight, like Mr. and Mrs. Johnson?"

"Sometimes, but usually there's just a lot of talk and not much action."

"Why?"

"Mostly because everyone is so focused on the little things they disagree about, that they overlook the bigger things that they agree on. The point of this game is to find the big things we agree on, and to do something about them."

"Do you disagree about something?"

"Well, we did. Your Uncle Leonard has a problem

Chapter 17

finding people to work at the plant, and while we've spent a lot of time gathering information on the problem, these past few months, we haven't been able to agree on what the problem is, or how big it is. But we talked with a lot of people about it, and figured out what we agree on in general."

"Now we need to talk with a lot of Grandpa's friends, who disagree a lot, so we're going to play the Alliance game with them. But your Aunt McKenzie's never played it before, and Uncle Leonard's only played it once or twice, so we're going to practice so we can get better."

Looking quite solemn, Dusty asked, "We're going to talk about Uncle Leonard's problem?"

"We're going to talk about how people who agree that they are being affected by a big problem can get together, talk about it, and then come up with a way to start working on it together. And we're going to write it on your drawing paper, if you don't mind."

"I don't mind."

George said, "OK, go to your 'quiet place,' while I explain the process." Dusty closed his eyes briefly and breathed slowly and deeply. George stood, stepped up to the easel, picked up a blue marker and said, "OK, the complete process will include the following steps," and wrote,

"The Past"
"The Present"
"Future"
"Common Ground"
"Action Planning"

Then George stepped back and said, "We've already discussed the past and present, and I think we have a pretty good idea how to present that to the Lyceum. But we need practice in the rest. So, today we're going to try to identify 'ideal future scenarios' and 'common ground'."

McKenzie asked, "What do you mean by 'ideal future

scenarios'?"

George replied, "Well, in this case it means that when people 'grow up' they're fully functional adults. They know what they need to know, and are able to do what they need to do, in order to function in our society. And, we'll identify what that is by brainstorming. Dusty?"

"Brainstorming?"

"It's a way of sharing ideas in which people say what comes into their heads, and the other people in the group listen without commenting or judging. There's no 'good' or 'bad'. Honey?"

Donna said, "I assume by 'know' you mean in their heart as well as in their head?" George nodded once and she said, "They need to know the difference between what is important and what is unimportant. And to know that, they have to hold their family and their community in their heart."

George flipped the top sheet over, revealing a blank one, wrote, "Ideal Future Scenarios," and under that, "Important, unimportant—family in heart," on the board and said, "Leonard?"

"Economic self-sufficiency."

George wrote, "Economic self-sufficiency," on the board and asked, "McKenzie?"

"Be able to communicate effectively."

George wrote, "Communicate effectively," on the board and said, "Dusty?"

Dusty cocked his head to one side, frowned and said, "Take care of children?"

George smiled and nodded and wrote, "Take care of children." Then he said, "And as for me, I'd say 'People need to be able to participate in governing their community.'"

George wrote, "Participate in community government," on the board and asked, "Anything else?

Leonard said, "They need to be able to respond crea-

Chapter 17

tively and effectively to unexpected challenges."

George wrote, "Creative and effective response to unexpected," on the board and asked, "McKenzie?"

McKenzie said, "Learn and relearn."

George smiled and nodded and wrote, "Learn and relearn," then asked, "Anything else?"

Donna replied, "They need to be able to focus on the future."

George wrote, "Focus on the future," then said, "And as for me, I'd say, 'Collaborate with others.'"

George stepped back and looked at the list:

"Important, unimportant—family in heart."

"Economic self-sufficiency"

"Communicate effectively."

"Take care of children."

"Participate in community government."

"Creative and effective response to unexpected."

"Learn and relearn."

"Focus on the future."

Collaborate with others."

Then George asked, "Are any of these similar enough that we can combine them? Leonard?

"'Family in heart' and 'Take care of children.' It seems to me that those could be combined somehow."

George nodded and said, "That sounds possible. Honey, Dusty, any suggestions on how to combine them?"

Donna said, "How about, 'Hold those you love in your heart, and take care of them'?"

George looked to Dusty and asked, "Dusty?"

"That's fine, Grandpa."

George wrote down the changes and asked, "Anything else? McKenzie?"

McKenzie said, "What about 'communication' and 'collaboration?'"

George replied, "Combine them? Sure. How about,

'communicate and collaborate with others?'"

"Anything else? No? OK, let's rate them. We're going to use a system called 'multivoting'. Each of us gets three votes. The first is worth five points, the second is worth three, and the third is worth one. Donna?"

When all of them had placed their votes, George tallied them, flipped the old sheet of paper over, revealing another clean white sheet and wrote the following:

What People Need to Be Able to Do When They Grow Up

"Hold those you love in your heart and take care of them—3"

"Economic self-sufficiency—7"

"Communicate and collaborate with others—8"

"Creative and effective response to unexpected—2"

"Learn and relearn—20"

"Focus on the future—5"

George stood back again, joining the others in gazing at the list. Leonard said, "It's a bit long. Don't we need to consolidate it next?"

George nodded and said, "Yes, into a 'values' statement."

McKenzie said, "How about removing 'Creative and effective'? It's sort of included in 'Learn and relearn' and 'Focus on the future'.

George nodded, said, "Any objections? No? OK." and crossed off "Creative and effective..."

George turned to the others and said, "This list represents what we want people to be able to do when they grow up. The question is, 'How do they learn how to do all this?' Here..." George beckoned to Dusty, tore the sheet of paper off the board, handed it to Dusty and said, "Tape this up where everyone can see it."

Chapter 17

Dusty scurried off, fetched some tape from George's desk, taped the list to the wall of the cardboard house, returned the tape, and scurried back to his chair. George picked up a black marker, said, "The next step is to look for obstacles to our goal. What is preventing us or restricting people from achieving the goal?

"Now, remember, at this point we're just gathering ideas and throwing them up on the board. We're not looking for good or bad ideas, just whatever comes to mind. Dusty?"

"Not enough hugs?"

"Aww..." George scooped up Dusty, gave him a big, long hug, and passed him to Donna. As the adults took turns hugging Dusty, a smiling George turned and wrote, "Not enough hugs," on the board.

Then George caught Donna's eye, glanced at the wall clock, and arched a brow. She nodded, returned Dusty to his chair, and left to call Elizabeth.

When the other adults had resettled, George said, "Now, keep in mind that this is not an 'education' problem. We know that because kids only spend 12% of their time at school, Dr. Glenn's characteristics of healthy people, and all the information we have about media messages. It proves that all parts of our society are involved. This is a media, health, government, education, business, and community problem. So, what we want to examine is the central problem, and the way that problem expresses in each area of society. For instance, what's behind the 'hug scarcity' problem? Leonard?"

"Well, it's not just hugs, of course; it's all types of interpersonal contact."

McKenzie added, "Feeling and demonstrating affection or relationship, which create a sense of 'being connected'."

George nodded and said, "OK, if there's a 'scarcity' of those types of interpersonal contacts which make us feel related or connected, then how would that work out as problems in... government?"

Leonard replied, "We wouldn't feel connected to it and participation would go down, which it has."

George said, "Right. But there are two parts to each of these, the individual and the group. For instance, how we relate or fail to relate with government, and how it relates with us."

Then George turned toward them again and asked, "And in media?"

McKenzie's eyes opened wide and she said, "Oh! It's the same thing. Readership at the paper, at all local papers, it's been falling for years."

George replied, "That's one effect, yes. And in health?"

Donna walked back into the room, with her brow furrowed and a portable phone in her hand and said, "All the psychological problems that grow out of isolation, feeling disconnected, the inability to feel related with others, with the environment—"

"Oh my...!" exclaimed Leonard, "That's Bruce!"

George bowed his head, sighed, raised his head and gazed at Leonard and said, "Yes, the inability to relate is one of the symptoms, and causes, of ADD and many of the other problems of our youth. That's why, in order to treat them successfully, you first have to identify and work with the root causes."

George glanced to Donna, and she shook her head and shrugged her shoulders, indicating that there'd been no answer. George frowned momentarily, turned back to the group and asked, "Now Leonard, how does that same problem, isolation and the inability to relate, work out in business?"

"Huh? Oh, in business? Well, you have the isolation or lack of communication within and outside of a business. Between the various departments, between the

Chapter 17

various generations of workers—we have four at Terra—
between the levels of employees, and between the business
and its suppliers, customers, and its community."

George said, "Very good. And in Education?"

McKenzie replied, "Well, the dual expression would
be in what is taught and how, and in how the students
relate with that. I mean, a lot of what we teach kids has
no relationship to what they'll really need or use in life,
and the kids don't feel related or connected to it. But of
course, there's a lot more to it than that."

George nodded and said, "Of course.

"Now, finally, how does it work out in Community?"

Donna said, "We build neighborhoods that have no
center, no connectedness between the people who live
there, and they grow up feeling isolated, without community support networks, and don't learn how to relate
with people."

George said, "Thank you, Dear," stood back from the
board, turned to the group and said, "There are three
major areas of difficulty which work out as problems in
the six social groups we've been discussing. In addition to
"relationship," there's "purpose," and "intelligent activity.""

Donna announced, "It's time for dinner.

George grinned and replied, "Right. We don't have
time to pursue the other three tonight, or the four sub-
sidiary areas of difficulty that grow out of them, but we
will explore them in depth with the Lyceum."

Donna asked, "McKenzie, Leonard, will you be joining us?"

McKenzie replied, "I'd be happy to. What can I do to
help?"

Leonard said, "Thank you, but I'd better be getting
home. It's Bruce's night to fix dinner, and they're expecting me."

Then he turned to George and said, "We got a lot

done today, I'd say we're almost ready to go public. When should we take it to the Lyceum?"

"Let's see," George looked at his calendar and said, "looks like the seventh. Come on, I'll walk with you to your car."

Leonard turned to the ladies and said, "Good night, Donna. Thanks McKenzie. We'll follow up next week?"

McKenzie waved and called, "Right. Looking forward to it, Leonard."

Following George's lead to the front door and outside, they stopped and stared in silence at the full moon that hung on the horizon."

"The moon and stars are fascinating, aren't they? Like the sun, they are shared by every human being on the planet," mused Leonard.

"So is the earth," George commented.

"I guess you're right."

Gazing up, George said, "Sometimes at night, on my way home from Terra, I would think about my job and how cool it was to be working for a company that was all about doing things for the earth. Then I'd go inside and have a cup of the dark cocoa and read a myth from one of the books in my collection. Well, last night, I did that very thing, but the book I picked up was a copy of *The Power of Myth* by Joseph Campbell, with Bill Moyers.

"I flipped it open, as I often do, and you know what I turned to?"

"I'm listening"

"It was his statement about a fourth function of mythology. He called it the pedagogical function of myth, of how to live a human lifetime under any circumstances. He said, 'myth can teach you that.'

"So, the old myths aren't being passed down and aren't working any more, and we need new ones?"

"Let's just say that he was pointing his readers in

Chapter 17

the direction of remembering their connections and dependency on the systems of the earth that support us all. He suggested that the new myths to come would be about our whole planet as an organism, with an emphasis on 'whole planet'. Kind of like the first astronauts who, gazing down after three days on their spaceship, said that the only thing they could see was the *whole* earth."

"So, are you saying we've taken up a task that's too big for us and we might do better to start with a story?"

"No and yes. Myths are born out of people's dreams, their images of the ideal they would like to achieve. I think we're in the early stages of building a new myth, building the foundation of a story about people rediscovering the value of their individual worth, within the context of the culture they live in. It's a huge saga that cries out for new, local stories with mythological potential.

"We seem to be in the right time and place to help people do that, to rediscover their potential for working together. It reminds me of the way people come to this country, and why. Regardless, Leonard, it's a task worthy of our time and our attention."

"And the next step in building or telling the myth is to take the story to the community," replied Leonard.

"That's right. At the next Lyceum meeting," said George.

"Good night Leonard."

"Good night, George, see you on the 7th."

Seeking the Soul of Commerce

Afterword

The System, Seeking the Soul of Commerce is a story with a three fold purpose.

The first was to share a story, a story of a community—like many communities across the nation and around the globe—who face issues where there are no easy solutions. In the community of Chantilly, the challenge was about creating a new generation of capable people with the critical, creative thinking skills necessary to be the innovators of the future. Everyone had a view of the problem and their own view of the solution. But until there was:

1. Agreement to integrate multiple and diverse motivations,
2. Development of a common understanding of words, and
3. Agreement on a set of expectations,

well intended people ended up at cross purposes.

In *The System, Seeking the Soul of Commerce*, we see many of the stakeholders that exist in our own communities. Looking from the outside in helps see the challenges from a community view point and thus helps us to rise "above the storm" to begin thinking with a new perspective.

The second purpose was to show how a community can begin the process of developing a set of shared values, shared language, shared motivations and ultimately a shared vision, using a set of tools that have a proven track record of bringing diverse stakeholders together. George, McKenzie, and Leonard start the process at the end of this volume of *The System*. Together they begin an action plan that brings them together.

Ultimately their actions will bring together all of the stakeholders, the community members of Chantilly, to create the workforce of the future. There are 6 key steps that they must follow in order to accomplish this. Those steps are:

1. Identify and attract stakeholder community leaders.
2. Agree on common language and a set of shared values.
3. Agree on a shared vision and measures of success.
4. Establish a plan including the stakeholder roles and responsibilities and the relationships or interfaces between stakeholders.
5. Agree on the resources, and source of those resources, to achieve the shared vision.
6. Establish and implement a management process for carrying out the plan. It should include a set of processes that track performance to the plan that includes measurement of cost, schedule, and achievement of key milestones, identification of risks and plans to address those risks, and ways to resolve issues

The third purpose of *The System, Seeking the Soul of Commerce* is to set the framework for volume II of *The System, "Finding the Soul of Commerce,"* in which all of Chantilly aligns around a shared vision. This next volume continues their story as they develop and implement the six step integrated action, with the Chantilly Lyceum as the forum. It is through this implementation that we find the soul of commerce and begin the transformation of the systems in Chantilly that create the new generation of critical and creative thinkers.

To Be Continued in:

The System,

Volume II

Finding the Soul of Commerce

Bibliography

Further information may be found in the following:

Books:

Bloom, Howard, *Global Brain*, The Evolution of the Mass Mind, John Wiley & Sons, 2000

Bohm, David, and Peat, David, *Science, Story & Creativity*, The Creative Roots of Science, Bantam Books, 1987

Campbell, Joseph, *The Power of Myth*, Doubleday, 1988 ed.

Csikszentmihalyi, Mihaly, *Flow*, the Psychology of Optimal Experience, Harper, 1990

Doman, Glen, *How to Multiply Your Baby's Intelligence*, Doubleday, 1983

Elkind, David, *Miseducation*, Preschoolers at Risk, Knopf, 1987

Finegold, David, 2002, *What Employees Really Want*: Designing Talent Strategies in an Age of Uncertainty, Drucker School of Management, Executive Forum Series, 2002.

Glenn, Stephen H., *7 Strategies for Developing Capable Students*, Random House, 1998

Glenn, Stephen H., *Raising Self-Reliant Children in a Self-Indulgent World*, Random House, 1998

Healy, Jane, *Endangered Minds*, Why Children Don't Think & What We Can Do About It, Touchstone, 1990

Kohn, Alfie, *Punished by Rewards*, Houghton-Mifflin, 1993

Needleman, Jacob, *The American Soul*, Penguin Group, 2003

Pearce, Joseph Chilton, *Magical Child*, Penguin Group, 1977

Pfeffer, J. & Sutton, R.I., *The Knowing-Doing Gap*, Harvard Business School Press, 1999

Quartz & Senjowski, *Liars, Lovers & Heroes*, What the New Brain Science Reveals About How We Become Who We Are, William Morrow, 2002

Weisbord, Marvin R., *Discovering Common Ground*, Barrett-Koehler Publishers, 1992

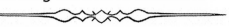
Reports:

Congressional Hearings, 2003, <u>Senate Government Affairs Subcommittee on Oversight of Government Management, the Federal Workforce and the District of Columbia Hold Hearings on Evaluating Human Capital at NASA</u>

Jonas, Donald K., Ph.D., 2002, <u>Workforce 2020: Trends Shaping the Future of Work</u>, A Keynote Presentation to the SME Annual Meeting

Education Insights at Public Agenda, <u>Are Parents and Students Ready for More Math and Science?</u> Reality Check 2006

The Institutes for the Achievement for Human Potential, <u>On Site Parenting Course: How to Multiply Your Baby's Intelligence,</u> 1978, Wyndmoor, PA 19038 www.iahp.org

www.gentlerevolution.org

The National Board on Education Testing and Public Policy, <u>The Education Pipeline in the United States 1970–2000</u>, January, 2004

National Center for Education Statistics, <u>The Averaged Freshman Graduation Rate for Public High Schools From the Common Core of Data, School Years 2001-02 and 2002-03,</u> October, 2005

National Center on Secondary Education and Transition, <u>Essential Tools</u>—Increasing Rates of School Completion, Moving From Policy and Research to Practice, A Manual for Policymakers, Administrators, and Educators, Part I, How are Dropout Rates Measured? What are Associated Issues? Minneapolis MN

Spitzer, Robert E., 2002, <u>Preparing Young Engineers for Industry,</u> A report to the American Society of Mechanical Engineers

U.S. Census Bureau, <u>School Enrollment in the United States</u>—Social and Economic Characteristics of Students, *Population Characteristics*, March, 2001

Magazine Online:

Engardio, Pete, Bernstein, Aaron, and Kripalani, with Balfour, Frederic (in Manila), Grow, Brian (in Atlanta) and

Bibliography

Greene, Jay, (in Seattle), 2003, The New Global Job Shift, a cover story for BusinessWeek/online,

Scott, William B., "People" Issues are Cracks in Aero Industry Foundation, Aviation Week and Space Technology, June 21, 1999 p. 63

Scott, William B., Systems Strategy Needed to Build Next Aero Workforce, Aviation Week and Space Technology, May 6, 2002, p. 61

Industries "Hire and Fire" Paradigm is Obsolete and New Management Incentives Are Key to Change, www.aviationnow.com, June 21, 1999

Video Tapes:

Glenn, Stephen, Developing Capable Young People, A taped presentation to the Quest National Skills for Learning Foundation Conference, 1982

Rushkoff, Douglas (Correspondent and Consulting Producer), Merchants of Cool, A PBS Video Presentation Frontline Series, 1999

http://www.futuresearch.net/

http://www.openspacetechnology.com/

Productive Workplaces—Organizing and Managing for Dignity, Meaning and Community, Marvin Weisbord, Jossey Bass, 1991

Discovering Common Ground, Marvin Weisbord (editor) Berret Kohler, 1992

Future Search—An Action Guide to Finding Common Ground in Organizations and Communities, Marvin Weisbord, Sandra Janoff, Berret Kohler, 1995

Open Space Technology—A User's Guide (second edition) Harrison Owen, Berret Kohler, 1997

Miscellaneous:

The Institutes for the Achievement for Human Potential, On Site Parenting Course: How to Multiply Your Baby's Intelligence, 1978, Wyndmoor, PA www.iahp.org

www.gentlerevolution.org

Bibliography

Printed in the United States
57828LVS00004B/1-51